Accidents and emergencies in childhood

*Papers based on a conference held
at the Royal College of Physicians*

Edited by
Jo Sibert
*Professor of Community Child Health
University of Wales College of Medicine*

1992

ROYAL COLLEGE OF PHYSICIANS OF LONDON

Acknowledgement

The publication of this book is made possible by the continuing and generous support of the Children Nationwide Medical Research Fund to whom the Royal College of Physicians is most grateful.

Royal College of Physicians of London
11 St Andrews Place, London NW1 4LE

Registered Charity No. 210508

Copyright © 1992 Royal College of Physicians of London
ISBN 1 873240 50 3

Typeset by Bath Typesetting Ltd, Bath, Avon
Printed in Great Britain by The Lavenham Press Ltd
Lavenham, Sudbury, Suffolk CO10 9RN

Preface

by R. Hugh Jackson MC OBE FRCP

President, Child Accident Prevention Trust, London

The choice of Accidents and Emergencies in Childhood for the 1991 Paediatric Conference of the Royal College of Physicians is an indication of the increased recognition that is being given to this aspect of child health. Indeed, considering the fact that accidents are by far the most common cause of death in childhood after the first nine months, and that—among other indices of their importance—they are the cause of over two million attendances at accident and emergency departments, it is surprising that hitherto they have not been accorded the concern that they deserve.

That this is so can in part be explained by the way that paediatrics has developed as a discipline. The early paediatricians tended to look at adult medicine as it applied to children, thence to aspects of growth and development and to branches of medicine which related entirely to children, such as neonatology. Trauma, being 'surgical' rather than 'medical', seldom came their way. Even with the development of child health clinics, accident prevention was seldom seen as an aspect of preventive medicine.

The earliest moves towards the prevention of accidents in childhood occurred when the health and safety of children in mines and factories became a public health responsibility. The virtual abolition of child labour in the UK and its replacement as a major cause of accident injury by burns and other accidents in the home or on the roads initially resulted in health professionals being concerned more with the management of injuries than their prevention.

However, paediatricians came to recognise their important role in accident prevention. This is illustrated in the proceedings of this conference which include the primary prevention of the accident itself, the secondary amelioration or prevention of the injuries sustained in the accident, and the tertiary management and rehabilitation of the injured child. The classic triad of factors relating to the child him- or herself, the causative agent for the injuries, and the environmental circumstances with which the child and the agent come into contact are also covered in the various papers. Second, the standard approaches to prevention, education, environmental engineering and legislation or regulation are discussed with emphasis on the multidisciplinary nature of accident and injury prevention. To complete the spectrum of injuries, the interface between child abuse and truly accidental injury is also examined.

There is still far to go in the field of accident and injury prevention. Hitherto, most of the effort in prevention has been put into education in the hope, not merely of increasing awareness of the danger of injuries, but also of changing adult and child behaviour. This, however, is a long-term process and indeed very difficult to evaluate. There is an increasing recognition of the effectiveness of making everyday objects safer and of reducing the risks to children in the environment inside the home, on the roads, and in the play and sports areas, supplemented where necessary by legislation and regulations. The role of health services must be to collect the data on the numbers and severity of the different types of injuries and the factors underlying them, and to use this information to decide the most appropriate interventions for specific injuries. As Professor Pless points out in his chapter, it is the ultimate way in which the effectiveness of accident prevention methods should be measured.

It is hoped that this book will raise the level of interest of child health doctors and others involved in the care of children in this vitally important field of medicine.

Contributors

A. W. Craft MD FRCP, *Consultant Paediatrician, Royal Victoria Infirmary, Newcastle-upon-Tyne; Department of Child Health, The Medical School, Newcastle-upon-Tyne NE2 4HH*

R. E. Cudmore MB ChB FRCS DCH DObstRCOG, *Consultant Paediatric Surgeon, Alder Hey Children's Hospital, Liverpool L12 2AP*

D. P. Davies BSc MD DObst RCOG DCH FRCP, *Department of Child Health, University of Wales College of Medicine, Cardiff CF4 4XN*

J. F. T. Glasgow MD FRCP, *Reader, Department of Child Health, The Queen's University of Belfast; Consultant Paediatrician, Accident and Emergency Department, Royal Belfast Hospital for Sick Children BT12 6BE*

A. J. Glasgow, *Medical Student, The Queen's University of Belfast BT12 6BJ*

H. R. M. Hayes PhD, *Technical Officer, Child Accident Prevention Trust, 18–20 Farringdon Lane, London EC1R 3AU*

C. J. Hobbs BSc MB BS MRCP(UK) DObstRCOG, *Consultant Community Paediatrician, St James's University Hospital, Leeds LS9 7TF*

A. Kemp MB MRCP, *Senior Registrar, Department of Child Health, University of Wales College of Medicine, Lansdowne Hospital, Cardiff CF1 8UL*

S. Levene MA MRCP, *Medical Consultant, Child Accident Prevention Trust, 18–20 Farringdon Lane, London EC1R 3AU*

I. B. Pless BA MD, *Professor of Pediatrics, Epidemiology and Biostatistics, McGill University; Director, Community Pediatric Research Program, McGill-Montreal Children's Hospital Research Institute, Montreal, Quebec H3H 1P3 Canada*

L. Polnay BSc MB BS FRCP DCH DObstRCOG, *Reader in Child Health, Queen's Medical Centre, University Hospital, Nottingham NG7 2UH*

J. R. Sibert MD FRCP DCH DObstRCOG, *Professor of Community Child Health, Department of Child Health, University of Wales College of Medicine, Lansdowne Hospital, Cardiff CF1 8UL*

A. N. P. Speight MA MB BChir FRCP DCH, *Consultant Paediatrician, Dryburn Hospital, Durham DH1 5TW*

S. Stewart-Brown PhD MFPHM MRCP(UK), *Consultant in Public Health Medicine, Worcester and District Health Authority WR4 9RW; Public Health Medicine Advisor, Hereford and Worcester Family Health Services Authority; Honorary Senior Lecturer, Department of Social Medicine, Birmingham University*

R Sunderland MD MRCP(UK), *Consultant Paediatrician, Selly Oak Hospital B29 6JD and Birmingham Accident Hospital*

Contents

1 | Accident prevention— environmental change and education

Alan Craft

Consultant Paediatrician, Royal Victoria Infirmary, Newcastle-upon-Tyne; Department of Child Health, The Medical School, Newcastle-upon-Tyne

Jo Sibert

Professor of Community Child Health, Department of Child Health, University of Wales College of Medicine, Lansdowne Hospital, Cardiff

The importance of accidents to children

In England and Wales accidents remain the commonest single cause of death in childhood between the ages of one and 15 years. They are more than twice as important as the next two causes, cancer and the late effects of congenital abnormalities. In 1990, 616 children died in England and Wales as the direct result of an accident.[1] Non-fatal accidents are also important as a cause both of immediate morbidity and of later disability. It has been estimated that 20% of all hospital admissions of children are a consequence of an accident, and that one in every five of the child population will attend an accident and emergency department each year. This means that, on average, any individual child will have an accident serious enough to require hospital treatment three times before he reaches his 15th birthday.[2] Although the rate of accidental death has fallen over the past 50 years, accidents have assumed a relatively greater importance because of the decline of other competing causes such as serious infections. There can be no doubt, therefore, that accidents are a major health problem and that their prevention should be a major public health issue.[3]

How can accidents be prevented?

How can accidental injury to children be prevented, and what is the role of the doctor? Doctors of many disciplines are in a unique position in society not only to observe and treat the injuries suffered by children but also to take the vital step of asking *why* the accident that caused the injury happened and whether anything can be done to prevent a recurrence. The prevention itself has traditionally been based on education, and for many years the effectiveness of this was completely unevaluated. When such scientific evaluation as was possible was undertaken, it was disappointing to learn that the vast majority of efforts and techniques which had been employed in the past were, at best, of little benefit and, at worst, actually harmful, increasing the rate of injury.

There then followed an era during which an attempt was made to understand better the whole accident process, to include the particular characteristics of the person involved, any other agent involved and the circumstances which led to the accident. From these studies the whole accident/injury cycle became more clear and alternative methods of prevention were suggested. Education had traditionally meant trying to alter the behaviour of a child likely to have the accident, but attempts at changing the environment proved more effective.

It would seem, therefore, that environmental change has a greater influence than education in preventing accidents, but the question whether there should be education *or* environmental change may be too simplistic. The real question is *how* to achieve this environmental change, and the concept of environmental change *by* education should perhaps be considered. This leaves the problem of *what* environmental changes are likely to be most effective and acceptable to the public, and *who* should be educated.

Prevention strategies

What is the evidence for the effectiveness of each of these strategies and how can they be employed to reduce this major epidemic which is now the major barrier between the first birthday and middle age?

Education

The temptation is to believe that the general public has a positive desire to prevent accidents and all that is required is to alert people to the dangers by means of education campaigns. The evidence that mass educational campaigns are effective is at best marginal. One of the problems encountered in reviewing the evidence for the effectiveness of education is that there have been very few attempts at evaluation, and even fewer controlled studies of intervention.

The Rockwood County Study in the USA was an attempt to look at education in an intervention and a reasonably close well-matched control area.[4] The importance of including a control was evidenced by the *rise* in the accident rate in both study and control areas after the putative intervention. It was possible to conclude, therefore, that education probably did no harm but was certainly not beneficial.

In the UK, the BBC has produced two major educational initiatives to try to prevent accidental injury. The *Play it safe* programmes were initially broadcast in 1980, and a new version has recently been screened in the UK (in 1992). An enormous amount of time, thought and money has been put into the production of these programmes, but the evaluation has been disappointing. Accident rates were not affected by the nationwide programmes, and at a more local level parents of small children took no action to improve the safety of their own homes even when encouraged by their health visitor specifically to watch the programmes.[5] However, if a programme was followed by a visit to the home by the health visitor to discuss child safety in the home, Colver and his colleagues showed that parents did take positive steps to make the home safer.[6] An education campaign in Cardiff using posters and literature sensitised parents to trivial accidents for which they sought help, but it did nothing to prevent such accidents.[7]

In Australia, a study looked at whether education could alter the attitudes of 12–14 year olds regarding safety. Factual knowledge was improved by the instigation of examinations, but unfortunately attitudes, and presumably therefore actions, did not alter.[8]

There is now some insight into why these various educational initiatives have not worked to lower the accident rate. One major factor is the involvement of psychosocial factors, for example, stress, in the aetiology of many childhood accidents. Stress has been found to relate to road traffic accidents,[9] accidental poisoning in children,[10] and accidents in general in young children.[11] In most of these it is stress within the family which is important, and it is easy to understand how traditional safety priorities can be disregarded under duress. For example, the mother who normally keeps medicines safely is confronted by a two-year-old at midnight with a fever. Her husband has just lost his job and come home intoxicated with alcohol. They live in a two-room house with two adults, three children and a dog. Is it any wonder that she leaves the paracetamol medicine by the child's bed after she has given him a dose?

Environmental change

If education alone is unhelpful, is there evidence that environmental change is any better? There are now many examples where an alteration to the environment, in its broadest sense, has shown itself to be effective not only in altering behaviour but also in reducing the toll of accidents.

Poisoning

Accidental poisoning in childhood is a good example of the steps necessary to bring about environmental change. It has been investigated in a sound methodological way. The circumstances of the poisoning incidents were initially well researched, not only discerning with what the child was poisoned but also exactly how it happened, for whom the medicine was originally prescribed or bought, and how it was stored. Traditionally, attempts at poisoning prevention have relied on education campaigns which aim to encourage people to keep their medicines safely, preferably in lockable cabinets, and to discard or return unused products. Research showed that both the hoarding of medicines and poor storage were important aetiological factors, and that even when lockable medicine cabinets were built into new homes they generally were not used for the purpose for which they were intended. These education campaigns were evaluated and found to be ineffective.[12,13] In addition, psychosocial stress was found to be important in the genesis of such incidents.[14]

Environmental change was, therefore, needed by means of a passive safety measure. Although the idea of child-resistant containers (CRC) was first suggested by Arena in North Carolina in 1959,[15] it took some time for them to be evaluated and brought into almost universal use. CRCs were evaluated in the USA by Scherz, and poisoning cases were reduced from 147 to 17 per year.[16] Following this successful field trial, they were introduced for aspirin preparations in the USA where they reduced poisoning episodes by 50%,[17] and in the UK by 75%.[18] In the UK, their use has now been extended to all medicines, this being a professional requirement of the Royal Pharmaceutical Society, and they are now also used on a variety of household products. In 1990, deaths from poisoning had been reduced to eight in England and Wales.

Road traffic accidents

Children as pedestrians are most at risk of injury from road traffic accidents. Research has shown that boys between five and eight years are at greatest risk. Such children are not able to estimate the danger or speed of traffic or to foresee dangerous situations.[19,20] A recent study of head injury has shown that 72% of deaths occurred between 3 and 9 pm, mostly to boys playing after they have left school. Traditional measures of road safety education do not seem to be effective, and even such standard techniques as 'kerb drill' and the Green Cross Code when evaluated seem to be less than adequate.[21] It seems likely that the only way to reduce such accidents is drastically to modify the environment to ensure that high-speed vehicles and children do not come into contact. Traffic speed can be reduced by 'sleeping policemen' and narrowing roads, but more drastic solutions are probably needed, such as that adopted in the Netherlands where the 'Woonerf' clearly identifies an area as residential where pedestrians, and in particular children, have absolute priority.[22]

Passengers in cars

Accidents to children in cars are not so important numerically as when they are pedestrians but their prevention has been somewhat easier. There is good evidence that the introduction of seat belts in 1983 for adults reduced serious injuries substantially, and there is now equally striking evidence for child restraint systems preventing both injury and death. In the UK, the Transport and Road Research Laboratory found that during a two-year period no child died whilst restrained in a car, whereas 264 were killed who were unrestrained.[23] Similar findings were seen in the USA.[24]

Bicycle accidents

There has been a steady fall in the number of children killed in bicycle accidents, with occasional interruptions. In the early 1960s and 1970s two new designs of bicycle were introduced, the small wheel and the 'high rise', the latter being especially designed and marketed with children in mind. Their appearance on the scene led to an abrupt increase in both injuries and deaths.[25] Manufacturers were alerted to the dangers and, although not admitting that their design was in any way to blame for the increase in injuries, they modified the styles to make them more stable and therefore safer. The wearing of helmets by older motorcyclists has significantly reduced severe head injury in accidents involving such road users. In view of the high risk of injury to the head in pedal cyclist accidents, it seemed sensible to try to introduce pedal cycle helmets. During any boy's childhood there is a one in 80 chance that he will be admitted to hospital with a serious head injury.[26] Unfortunately, cycle helmets have been expensive and not attractively designed, so that fashion-conscious young people will not use them. However, this situation seems to be improving, and helmet use is now being actively encouraged in some areas.[27]

Drowning

Drowning is more important in countries with a warm climate, with many outdoor swimming pools and where water recreation is a common pastime. However, even in England and Wales approximately 50 children die by drowning each year. There is no doubt that supervision of children in public swimming pools has reduced them as places of drowning fatalities, with none in 1988.[28] In Australia, drowning is a problem in unfenced private swimming pools. After the failure of education to reduce the toll of accidents many cities have introduced regulations to ensure adequate safe fencing of such pools, with a tenfold reduction in drownings.[29]

Burns and scalds

Patrick Brontë, the father of the Brontë sisters, was one of the first to recognise the problem of deaths from burns caused by flammable night-dress material. Each year he buried many such children in the churchyard in Howarth, Yorkshire. By bringing this local matter to the attention of the public in a letter to the local newspaper, a chemist suggested that impregnation of material with alum could make it flame-resistant. Thus, flame-proof night-dresses were produced—one of the first examples of environmental change being used to prevent injury. At the present time the most serious thermal injuries come from house conflagrations, and very often smoke as much as the heat causes death and injury.

Foam-filled furniture is a particular hazard, and after a successful Parliamentary lobbying campaign the regulations were changed in 1988 to make such furniture illegal. However, this is only for *new* furniture, and for many years to come homes will contain such lethal items. Education has been shown to be ineffective in influencing behaviour regarding fire safety.[30] Passive safety measures are available in the form of effective smoke alarms, and should now be recommended for every home.[31]

Conclusions

The above are a few examples of passive safety measures resulting in environmental change, which have been shown to lower the accident and injury rates significantly. It would seem, therefore, that environmental change is more effective than education, but two problems remain. Is there any role for general safety education of the public and, secondly, whom should we be educating to bring about environmental change? The solutions to both these questions are linked. There seems little doubt that education of the public can bring about a better general safety awareness which, if inculcated in children from an early age, should hopefully raise successive generations who are more aware of safety matters. Direct education of the designers and maintainers of the environment is important, but if those who are subsequently to become architects, designers or engineers grow up with and within a safety conscious ethos it is much more likely that a social change will be brought about through evolution. It is now recognised that the best hope to prevent tobacco smoking is by changing attitudes in the young, and the same is almost certainly true of safety.

Improvements in accident rates will be slow and will come about as a result of environmental change *by* education. Both are needed, but the education needs to be correctly targeted. The doctor undoubtedly has a role to play in this change.[32]

References

1. Office of Population Censuses and Surveys. Deaths by accidents and violence. *Quart Monitors DH4 Series*. London: OPCS, 1988
2. Sibert JR, Maddocks GB, Brown M. Childhood accidents—an endemic of epidemic proportions. *Arch Dis Child* 1981; **56**: 2–7
3. Child Accident Prevention Trust. *Basic principles of child accident prevention*. London: CAPT, 1989
4. Schlesinger ER, Dickson DG, Westaby J, Logrillo VM, Maiwald AA. A controlled study of health education in accident prevention: the Rockland County child injury project. *Am J Dis Child* 1966; **111**: 490–6
5. Sibert JR, Williams H. Medicine and the media. *Br Med J* 1983; **286**: 1893
6. Colver AF, Hutchinson PJ, Judson EC. Promoting children's home safety. *Br Med J* 1982; **285**: 1177–80
7. Minchom P, Sibert JR. Does health education prevent childhood accidents? *Postgrad Med J* 1984; **60**: 260–2
8. Whitelaw S. Evaluation of educational projects in Australia. In: Manciaux M, Romer CJ, eds. *Accidents in childhood and adolescence*. Geneva: World Health Organisation, 1991:161
9. Backett EM, Johnston AM. Social pattern of road accidents to childhood. Some characteristics of vulnerable families. *Br Med J* 1959; **i**: 403–9
10. Sibert JR. Stress in families of children who have ingested poisons. *Br Med J* 1975; **iii**: 87–9
11. Brown GW, Davidson S. Social class, psychiatric disorder of mother and accidents to children. *Lancet* 1978; **i**: 378–81
12. Harris DW, Karindiker DS, Spencer MG, Leach RH, Bower AC, Mander GA. Returned medicines campaign in Birmingham 1977. *Lancet* 1979; **ii**: 599
13. Ferguson DM, Horwood LJ, Beautrais MA, Shannon FT. A controlled trial of a poison prevention method. *Pediatrics* 1982; **69**: 515
14. Bithoney WG, Snyder J, Michalek J, Newberger EH. Childhood ingestions as symptoms of family distress. *Am J Dis Child* 1986; **139**: 456–9
15. Arena JM. Safety closure caps. *JAMA* 1959; **169**: 1187–8
16. Scherz RG. Prevention of childhood poisoning. *Pediatr Clin North Am* 1970; **17**: 713
17. Clarke A, Walton WW. Effect of safety packaging on aspirin ingestion by children. *Pediatrics* 1979; **63**: 687–93
18. Sibert JR, Craft AW, Jackson RH. Child resistant packaging and accidental child poisoning. *Lancet* 1977; **ii**: 289–90
19. Howarth CI, Routledge DA, Repetto-Wright R. An analysis of road accidents involving child pedestrians. *Ergonomics* 1974; **17**: 319–30
20. Kohler L, Ljungblom B-A. *Child development and traffic behaviour. Traffic and children's health*. Stockholm: Nordic School of Public Health, 1987

21. Grayson GB. The identification of training objectives: what shall we tell the children? *Accid Anal Prevent* 1981; **13**: 169–73
22. Royal Dutch Touring Club. *Woonerf*. The Hague, Netherlands: Royal Dutch Touring Club, 1977 (Available from: Royal Dutch Touring Club, PO Box 93200, The Hague, Netherlands)
23. Transport and Road Research Laboratory. *The protection of children in cars (Leaflet 345)*. Crowthorne, Berkshire: TRRL, 1974
24. Scherz RG. Restrain systems for the prevention of injury to children in automobile accidents. *Am J Public Health* 1976; **66**: 451
25. Craft AW, Shaw DA, Cartlidge NEF. Bicycle injuries in children. *Br Med J* 1973; **112**: 146–7
26. Clarke AJ, Sibert JR. Why child cyclists should wear helmets. *Practitioner* 1986; **230**: 513–4
27. Walker A. Cycling in cities. *Br Med J* 1990; **301**: 80
28. Kemp A, Sibert JR. *Drowning and near drowning in children*. Proceedings of the 62nd Annual Meeting of the British Paediatric Association, Warwick, 1990
29. Pearn JH, Nixon J. Are swimming pools becoming more dangerous? *Med J Aust* 1977; **2**: 702–4
30. McCabe M, Moore H. Is national fire safety week a waste of time? *Fire Prevent* 1990; **232**: 12–4
31. US Fire Administration. *An evaluation of residential smoke detectors under actual field conditions (Final Report EMW-C-002)*. Washington, DC: US Fire Administration, 1980
32. Sibert JR. Accidents to children: the doctor's role; education or environmental change. *Arch Dis Child* 1991; **66**: 890–3

2 | Local and community approaches to child accident prevention

Sarah Stewart-Brown

Consultant in Public Health Medicine, Worcester and District Health Authority
Public Health Medicine Advisor, Hereford and Worcester Family Health Services Authority
Honorary Senior Lecturer, Department of Social Medicine, Birmingham University

Introduction

Accident prevention is prone to partitioning with respect to:

- causes (home, road traffic and occupational accidents);
- injury (burns, falls, drownings, ingestions);
- people (children, elderly, young people); and
- prevention:
  - road safety officers work at district councils;
  - professionals in burns units develop burn and scald prevention programmes;
  - paediatricians develop programmes to prevent ingestions; and
  - surgeons develop programmes to prevent head injury.

Accident preventers are also prone to division into those who:

- favour environmental change;
- believe that legislation is the answer;
- work to achieve behaviour change.

The 'community approach' to accident prevention uses a more holistic approach. One of its key goals is a general shift in the community's attitude to risk-taking behaviour. It works by supporting the community to the stage at which people believe that accidents are *not* inevitable and can be controlled. There is no conflict between this and other methods of accident prevention; they are complementary and reinforce each other.

What is a community approach to accident prevention?

The simplest definition of a community approach to accident prevention is: 'getting everyone in the community to work together towards a common goal'. It needs to be distinguished from community develop-

ment; this is one specific type of community approach to health
promotion which may or may not be a component of community
accident prevention projects. Community development is based on the
recognition that people need to feel in control of their own lives before
they embark on health-related behavioural changes. In the social
groups most at risk of accidents such feelings cannot be taken for
granted. It works by empowering communities and the individuals
within them to tackle any health and social concerns they may have
(like accidents), and by supporting their efforts to change things for
the better.

In the past the health service has not been very good at recognising
that empowerment is an essential part of health promotion. This can
be illustrated by quoting from a study in the north of England in the
late 1970s on women's attitudes to the child health services. Many
women felt that the service undermined their confidence.[1] The following quote is typical of the feelings of many of those interviewed:

> I'm not so keen on going to the clinic. When I went with Gary, he'd got
> this rash on his face and she said to me 'go and show him to the doctor'.
> They make you feel as though you are not looking after them properly,
> they make you feel 'what am I doing wrong?'

A community action prevention project: the various steps

Embarking on a community accident prevention project can be
daunting. It is important to work with a multisectoral group, but
such groups are prone to do a lot of talking about accident prevention
and fail to take action. Setting up such a group will therefore not
necessarily get a project started.

Step 1: local statistics

An essential ingredient in getting started is local statistics on accidents.
These can provide the necessary motivation to take action. I am both
proud and embarrassed to present some information about accidents
in Worcester, proud because it is the culmination of two years' hard
work, and embarrassed because it has not been achieved with the
apparent effortlessness reported in other chapters (so characteristic
of the Newcastle Department of Child Health). It has not been
possible to use the accident and emergency department's computer to
collect and analyse the cause- and location-specific data essential to
accident prevention. In 1990, a retrospective review was carried out of
a random sample of accident and emergency department records at all
the casualty departments in the district. The casualty departments in

hospitals in neighbouring districts were also visited to assess the extent of outward cross-boundary flow. The latter was relatively insignificant for the majority of residents and, for those where there was a significant attendance, the effect did not influence our conclusions.

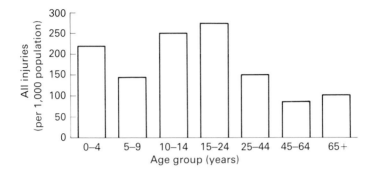

Fig. 1. *All injuries 1990, age-specific rates, Worcester and District Health Authority.*

Figure 1 shows age-specific injury rates for all district residents. The 15–24 year age group is most at risk of injury, followed by the 10–14 year olds and the under-5s.

Injuries in this study were grouped into four grades of severity.

- *major* injuries, which were potentially life-threatening;
- *moderate* injuries, which required expert treatment, for example, fractures of the long bones and burns or scalds either full thickness or between 1% and 10% of the body surface;
- *minor* injuries, those that required treatment such as suturing;
- *trivial* injuries which only required treatment which could be provided by non-professional people in the home. Nine out of ten attendances were generated by injuries of a minor or trivial nature.

Severe and moderate injuries Figure 2 shows the age-specific attendance rates for moderate and severe injuries. The 15–24 age group and the over-65s assume greater importance here and the under-5s rather less. This pattern is even more pronounced in Fig. 3 which shows death rates by age group. Although clearly the 15–24 year age group is most at risk of injuries of all levels of severity, it receives the least in the way of preventive health services. The health service component of the latter is targeted almost exclusively at the under-5s. This approach seems to have more to do with established patterns of service delivery than with patterns of risk.

Attendance rates Geographical analysis of injury attendances by people living in different parts of the district show that town dwellers are

almost twice as likely as people living in the country to attend an
accident and emergency department wih an injury. There was also a
twofold difference in attendance rates by residents of different towns
both for adults and for children (Fig. 4). The differences may be due to
different patterns of service usage rather than to true differences in the
rate at which people injure themselves. Nevertheless, given this information, it would be reasonable to propose that a community-based
prevention project should be established in Evesham, Pershore or
Worcester before one in Malvern or Droitwich.

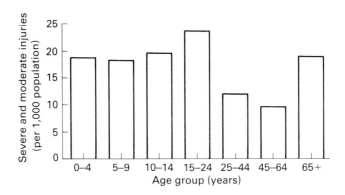

Fig. 2. *Severe and moderate injuries 1990, age-specific rates, Worcester and District Health Authority.*

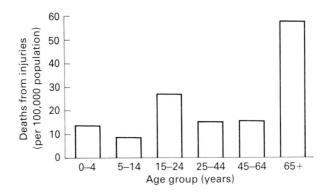

Fig. 3. *Injury death rates 1986–1990 by age group, Worcester and District Health Authority (1988 population-based).*

Step 2: causes of accidents

The largest group of injuries, both severe and less severe, in all towns
was accidents in the home. For severe and moderately severe injuries,

the next biggest group was road accidents, and for the less severe injuries, accidents at work. Less than half the records examined contained any information about the mechanism of injury, so it was not possible to develop a profile of the precise causes.

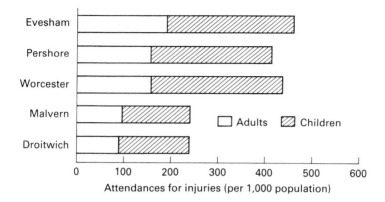

Fig. 4. *Attendance rates for injury in towns 1990, Worcester and District Health Authority.*

The next step in establishing a community-based accident prevention programme is to consider the causes of accidents in the widest sense and some of the broader issues. If it is possible to collect information about cause and place, this can be considered at the same time.

There are three distinct views on the causes of accidents in childhood. In any multisectoral accident prevention group all three views are likely to be held by some members.

The first view is that:

> Accidents happen because parents are not well informed, not sufficiently competent and do not have the right safety equipment.

This view epitomises what would appear to have been the traditional health professional's view of accident cause. It is based on the belief that parents can control the injury risks to which children are exposed, and that childhood injuries are primarily caused by parental incompetence.

The second is the kind of view that tends to be expressed by people working in deprived communities with high accident rates. People who feel this way believe that behaviour change by parents is ineffective in the absence of a change in the social and physical environment in which children are raised:

> How is it that under the most unpropitious circumstances most parents manage to keep their children safe most of the time?[2]

A third view which is frequently expressed is the fatalistic one, that accidents are an inevitable part of growing up, and even that risk taking should be encouraged as part of normal development. Courting danger is undoubtedly a cause for admiration in some sectors of society, but distinction can and should be drawn between the sort of risk taking which is dangerous and that which is essential for participation in society. The prospect of solving the accident problem by withdrawing children from participating in society must be avoided.

As an early step in an accident project on a council estate in Worcester the mothers of two pre-school children were given a camera and asked to photograph accident risks in their local community. They came back with a series of slides which showed that they were well aware of local accident risks. They may not have spotted all the risks, and were not always able to put them in the right order of priority for danger, but they found a lot of problems. They also clearly cared about keeping their children safe. Such observations have been made in community-based accident prevention projects elsewhere.

If parents are aware of risks, why do they go on living with them? The closer 'accident preventers' get to people who live in deprived communities the more reasons they are able to give. For example, mothers may find that things which might cause problems in the future, like not having a stair gate, are easier to ignore than things, like non-payment of the electricity bill, which inevitably will. Imposing an accident risk on children may actually be the safest thing to do in certain circumstances: if the man of the house comes home having had one too many drinks and in an aggressive mood, it could be less dangerous for the children to be out playing unsupervised on the street than it is for them to be 'safely' inside the house. It is sometimes difficult for health professionals living their relatively privileged lives to make judgements about how sensible or stupid is other people's behaviour. This is not to say that health professionals should not point out accident risks to parents, only that it is important to be sensitive to the reasons why children may be so exposed.

Step 3: involvement of the local community

After discussion about local statistics and consideration of the causes of accidents, it should be possible for colleagues in a multisectoral group to agree on a programme which addressess the district priorities, and which is practical given the resources available. The next stage is to win over prominent members of the targeted community. In Worcester, by presenting the statistics collected, we would hope to win over the health professionals (general practitioners, health visitors, community nurses and managers), local businesses, the town council, the heads of secondary and primary schools, playgroup leaders, community workers, the local safety groups like the Red Cross and St John Ambulance and, last but not least, the local newspaper reporters and radio station presenters.

If we get it right, I would expect the general public to start asking what they can do. The next steps would be determined by what was thought useful and would work. It might be possible to get schools to do projects documenting accident risk in the community, parents to police environmental risks to pre-schoolers, and the newspapers to publish month-by-month accident statistics. With sufficient training all prominent members of the community could become 'accident prevention' educators.

Resources would need to be invested to achieve this. The project would need a leader and many of those working in the community for the public services, in voluntary organisations, private businesses and in the home would need to be prepared to contribute some of their time. To obtain this sort of commitment, it would be necessary to demonstrate more than just faith that the project will work. Fortunately, there are now studies which have evaluated community accident projects and demonstrated positive benefit. In this country, community projects have succeeded in getting old, dangerous playgrounds demolished and new ones built, window locks fitted in council house flats, and holiday play schemes set up.[3]

Swedish project

The community accident prevention project which is probably the best documented was a large project based on Falköping, a town in Sweden (Fig. 5).[4] Rates of injury at all levels of severity and for different causes fell significantly in this town in comparison with those in the neighbouring town of Lidköping following a three-year project at the end

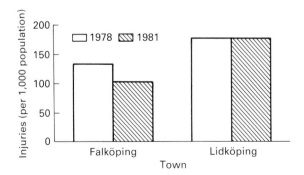

Fig. 5. *Swedish community intervention project.*

of the 1970s. In addition, it was possible to document a change in knowledge and attitudes to accident prevention in the community. There was a lot of newspaper coverage of prevention issues. Safety equipment was promoted in shops, and accident risks in the community challenged. This study is not the final word in demonstrating that community-based accident prevention can work. More studies are needed covering different approaches, and projects with different levels of resourcing. Nevertheless, the results of the Swedish study should provide enough encouragement to those who are considering embarking on such an initiative in the near future to help them get started.

References

1. Graham H. Women's attitudes to the child health services. *Health Visitor* 1979; **52**: 175–8
2. Roberts H, Corkerhill F & MAD Project. Public Health Research Unit, University of Glasgow
3. Child Accident Prevention Trust. *A training resource for health visitors*. London: Health Education Authority, 1991
4. Schelp L. Community intervention and changes in accident pattern in a rural Swedish municipality. *Health Promotion* 1987; **2**: 109–25

3 | The role of the Child Accident Prevention Trust

Sara Levene

Medical Consultant, Child Accident Prevention Trust, London

Introduction

This chapter considers a positive aspect of child safety, the work of the Child Accident Prevention Trust (the Trust). It outlines some of the thinking which led to the establishment of the Trust, its ways of working and examples of its past and present work. It also demonstrates some of its achievements, though they are subtle and often difficult to quantify.

The Trust was founded in 1978 by Dr Hugh Jackson, a Newcastle paediatrician. He had the practical career experience of seeing injured children admitted to hospital wards, and realised that many of the injuries might have been prevented, either by the removal of predictable dangers or with the use of relevant safety measures. At that time, existing safety organisations such as the Royal Society for the Prevention of Accidents could not adequately promote child safety. They were not in a position to cut across the divisions of safety, such as road safety and home safety, to view child safety as a special issue.

Childhood accidents

Child safety is a problem that cuts right across subject boundaries. Accidents that happen to children are not just related to their surroundings and their environment, but are intimately related to the children themselves.

First, they are linked to their physical development. It is best illustrated by taking a particular example, such as falls. A tiny baby can fall only if it is dropped or if an adult falls with the baby in her arms. Within a few months, the baby can wriggle and roll, and can fall if left on a high surface such as a bed or a table. Soon the baby can crawl and move itself into danger, for example, on the stairs. Gradually, the baby becomes a toddler who can climb and fall, and then a child who can fall outside the home, for example, from playground equipment or from a tree. This pattern of change in circumstances with age is repeated for many accident types.

17

Accidents are also linked to the child's intellectual development. A baby may scald itself by grabbing a hot drink. It will not learn not to do it again, let alone develop the concept of 'hot'. A five-year-old cannot judge the speed of oncoming cars. On the other hand, he does know that washing powder is not food, and is unlikely to swallow any on purpose.

A third link is to the normal emotional behaviour and growth of the child. Children play and explore. They range outside the home, climb fences and trees, and concentrate on the game in hand and not on the traffic nearby. Children are not small adults. They must be understood on their own terms. Their development and behaviour can be anticipated, and safety measures provided before they are required.

Anticipation of accidents

The aspect of anticipation also underlines the Trust's view of childhood injury as a medical problem as amenable to research as any other issue in public health. Accidents are not inevitable acts of God; they may be unexpected but, if they are studied, their context can be understood and, to some extent, be predicted—or, at least, high-risk situations be identified. Preventive measures can then be put into effect. Proper research also enables useful preventive measures to be distinguished from gimmicks, and preventive action to be targeted to the most relevant groups.

The Child Accident Prevention Trust

The Trust was needed to tackle children's accidents by combining an overview of the developing child with an understanding of the value of research and particular areas where it was most needed. The Trust is a registered charity. It receives some Department of Health funding, but this covers only a portion of its work. Funding for individual projects comes from various government departments, the Health Education Authority and grant-giving trusts as well as commercial sponsors. The trust remains clearly independent from any funders, and reports what it thinks, not what they want.

Research

An essential activity of the Trust is the pursuit of research. Equally important is the dissemination of research results. This does not just mean the production of a paper for a medical journal or for use in-house, but to put any results and recommendations in front of an audience which might act on them. This can be at the level of practitioners working with children and carers, and also at management, government or even European level.

Working parties

Trust working parties exemplify its view of child safety as a multi-sectoral problem. These groups are concerned to discuss particular issues, for example the safety of children in cars.[1] They meet at intervals over a period of one or two years to produce an expert report. Every attempt is made to ensure that all relevant fields are represented from the inception of the meetings and that a wide variety of expertise is contributed from the start. Members may be brought in from such widely differing sectors as industry, government, the police, the fire service and the medical profession. Disagreements are raised and contentious issues discussed within the working party. This enables the final report to deal with problems, and to produce a consensus opinion that is likely to meet with widespread acceptance, rather than a report which comes up against unforeseen issues and obstacles. The members from the different sectors are also an asset in that they promote the published report within their own fields.

Publications

Trust publications include accessible versions of various more technical reports, and a twice-yearly newsletter circulated to over 6,000 individuals with an interest or professional role in child safety. Every attempt is made to get these publications where they matter, which may be through sponsorship, so that free copies can be circulated, and through widespread distribution of flyers, particularly in the professional press.

Meetings

The Trust organises meetings on various child safety issues. These may be formal lectures, possibly by visiting foreign experts, lectures in conference format, possibly on an international scale, or workshops in which individuals can participate more fully.

Consultative role

Finally, the Trust has a consultative role. This includes representation on a number of safety standard committees, both in the UK and in Europe, and the provision of advice to members of the public, professional people such as health visitors and trading standards officers, and organisations such as the Department of Trade and Industry or commercial firms.

The work of the Trust

The work of the Trust falls under a variety of headings. The first can loosely be called 'injuries and intervention'. It is not possible to recommend any injury prevention measures without some background research. First, the incidence must be defined. How do most of the injuries occur, to children of what sex, age and family and social circumstances? Are there particular products or environmental features at fault? What remedial measures can be suggested, and have any of them been evaluated, either by intervention studies or on an ergonomic basis?

In this way, it is possible to answer two questions:

- what are the priorities for prevention?
- what interventions are worth recommending?

Prevention priorities and worthwhile interventions

An example is the report on burn and scald accidents.[2] Deaths from house fires are the single most common cause of child death in the home. Frequently, children cannot be evacuated from a burning building and are often found to have been asphyxiated in their sleep by fumes from the fire rising to bedrooms. Primary preventive measures, such as care with smokers' materials, could stop the fire. Match-resistant furnishings and combustion-modified foam are now required by law. But secondary preventive measures, to reduce the harm if fire does break out, such as smoke detectors which give early warning, can save lives. Intervention studies elsewhere suggest that smoke detectors are of real value, and evidence is now accumulating that they are working in the UK.[3,4]

On the other hand, proper study can reveal measures which are less effective. Scalds cause serious injury, particularly to toddlers, and a common cause is a child reaching for a pan on the stove. A cooker guard is a popular household safety item, but ergonomic evaluation points to problems with it:

- the guard has gaps for a child's fingers to reach the hob or gas flame;
- it is difficult to lift full pans over the guard.

They are an expensive and unsatisfactory solution, and the Trust does not recommend their use either in private homes or in the premises of child-minders or nurseries.

Practice and implementation

In the practice and implementation of safety measures sometimes obstacles may arise of management and planning. Health or local authorities may not have perceived the importance of childhood injury, and may have no idea about its epidemiology or the types of prevention approaches to try. This is why the Trust has produced a book, *Basic principles of child accident prevention*,[5] accompanied by a video,[6] which does not give solutions but tries to raise the issue. Both the book and video have been aimed at health and local authority managers and politicians, to whom it has been widely distributed. Other work aimed at what could be described as the political side of the issue is a study of the costs of injuries. This is the Trust's 'top-down' approach to promoting child accident prevention as an issue.

Campaigning and training

It is one thing to assess injuries or products and to develop idealised solutions to safety problems, but it is another matter to look at real-life situations to see how these solutions can be made to work. This involves campaigning and training. The difficult problems may some-times be social issues. There is a well-marked social gradient in accidental injury, and more dramatically in accidental death.[5] The solutions which work for middle-class home-owning parents may be inappropriate for less affluent families, who do not care any less about their children's safety but who have many more and other problems to contend with. It is even more inappropriate to fail to listen to less advantaged families. What are their safety concerns, and what safety strategies do they now have? What sort of measures would be useful and welcomed by them? A 'bottom-up' approach is needed as well as the 'top-down' one. The Trust has already taken a special interest in families living in temporary accommodation.[7] It is considering how other forms of safety services could be made consumer friendly. An example is the public access poisons information service, which would enable any individual, not just medical practitioners, to obtain telephone advice on the management and prevention of accidental poisoning.

It is easy for me to give worthy advice about listening to families, trying to meet their needs and working with them for child safety.[8] I do not work with families on a day-to-day basis, tackling local issues and local problems. Special skills are needed to put safety across at grass-roots' level. The Trust has attempted to fill this need in at least two ways. Two major projects have come to fruition in 1991.

1. The Approaches to Local Child Accident Prevention Project (ALCAPP).[9] This has drawn together all sorts of information about who is doing what in child accident prevention, what they are

doing and where they are working. The outcome is a database which can link together workers in the same profession, people in the same geographical area, or groups trying to tackle the same sorts of issues.
2. A set of publications which provides an overview of local work, a 'who's who' of child accident prevention, and some practical guidance on setting up an accident prevention group and carrying out certain types of work.

The Trust takes a special interest in the work of health visitors. They build relationships with client families, they visit their homes and see their problems. They are seen as a valuable source of advice because they have a good background knowledge of child development and how injuries occur. In an initial study the Trust was able to examine their role, training and the problems they encounter.[10] Health visitors may not fully understand the importance of child injury as a problem, and may find it very difficult to put safety issues across without seeming to be didactic or bullying. Worse, parents may misinterpret safety education as suspicion of child abuse.

With the help of the Community Education Development centre, the Trust has developed the health visitors' training resource.[11] This helps health visitors to improve their skills in dealing with child safety through imaginative exercises and an interactive video.[12] The approach of this work is through active participation, and differs completely from the passive lecture format traditional in medical teaching.

Conclusions

What has the Trust achieved? It would be simple to say 'so many lives have been saved' or 'so many injuries prevented', but it is not possible to quantify the work in this way, although deaths have been reduced. A strategic approach has been adopted. We have thought about what needed to be done, what people wanted, and have tried to pursue it, often choosing planners or politicians to participate in the process. To disseminate ideas to the public, the best use of the Trust resources is to go to professionals who work at grass-roots' level, rather than adopting a mass educational approach. We can help one another in this sort of work by providing contacts and information. The Trust has a resource centre with papers and books on all aspects of child safety. If the tiny secretariat does not have an expert in the field, one can be supplied. The ALCAPP database can be used to link people together, and various 'how to do it' guides be provided.

The Trust cannot act in isolation. The medical profession as a whole needs to recognise the importance of the child safety problem, and to take an active part in local initiatives as previously described. The BBC has made a series of programmes, *Play it safe*, about child safety, and a major national campaign is in place for 1992 and 1993. A television series alone may be able to do little to reduce childhood injuries, but it can sensitise people to the safety messages from health workers or other professionals. This is a particularly opportune time for doctors to share in the work of the Trust and promote child safety.

References

1. Child Accident Prevention Trust (CAPT). The safety of children in cars. *Occasional paper OP9*. London: CAPT, 1988
2. CAPT. *Burn and scald accidents to children*. London: Bedford Square Press, 1985
3. US Fire Administration. An evaluation of residential smoke detectors under actual field conditions. *Final report EMW-C-002*. Washington DC: US Fire Administration, 1980
4. Gorman RL, Charney E, Holtzman NA, Roberts KB. A successful city-wide smoke detector giveaway program. *Pediatrics* 1985; **75**: 14–18
5. CAPT. *Basic principles of child accident prevention*. London: CAPT, 1989
6. CAPT. *Child safety is no accident (video)*. London: CAPT, 1988
7. CAPT. *Safe as houses*. London: CAPT, 1991
8. CAPT. *You can't watch them 24 hours a day*. London: CAPT, 1991
9. CAPT. *Approaches to local child accident prevention*. London: CAPT, 1991
10. Laidman P. Health visiting and preventing accidents to children. *Health Education Authority research report no. 12*. London: Health Education Authority, 1987
11. Health Education Authority. *Preventing accidents to children: a training resource for health visitors*. London: CAPT, Health Education Authority, 1991
12. Health Education Authority. *Preventing accidents to children (video)*. London: CAPT, Health Education Authority, 1991

4 | The causes and prevention of falls

Michael Hayes

Technical Officer, Child Accident Prevention Trust, London

Introduction

Falls, like most childhood accidents, are a part of everyday life and happen to ordinary people going about their usual business which, in the case of children, is playing and moving about. All falls will never be prevented—it would be idealistic to think that they could be. What must be done is, first, to identify those falls that cause death, serious injury or disability, or can be easily prevented, regardless of their severity and, secondly, to ensure that a balance is struck between the need to protect and children's needs for a stimulating life-style, an essential part of growing up.

Epidemiology of falls

Fatal falls

In 1989, there were 27 fatal falls in England and Wales involving children under 15 years, 3.7% of the 722 accidental paediatric deaths in that year (Table 1).[1] The male to female ratio of 1.7 to 1 was slightly lower than the ratio for all accidental deaths for which it was 2.1 to 1.

Table 1. Deaths due to falls by age group, sex and location, England and Wales, 1989

| Location | Sex | Age group (years) | | | Total |
		< 1	1–4	5–14	
Home	M	1	3	4	8
	F	1	4	1	6
Other	M	—	1	8	9
	F	—	—	4	4
Total	M	1	4	12	17
	F	1	4	5	10

25

The data show that the younger children tend to have their accidents at home, while the fatalities among children over five tend to be elsewhere. This divergence can no doubt be linked with their change of life-style and range of movement as they grow older.

Falls ranked fifth behind transport accidents, drownings, inhalation, ingestion and suffocation, and deaths caused by fire and flames as a cause of accidental death in 1989. The breakdown of these falls by type of fall and age group is presented in Table 2. Although the numbers for one year are too small to allow firm patterns to be identified, they illustrate the role of falls from buildings and structures and from one level to another, especially among older children.

Table 2. Deaths due to falls by age group and type of fall, England and Wales, 1989

| ICD code | Type of fall | Age group (years) | | | |
		< 1	1–4	5–14	Total
E880	On or from stairs or steps	—	—	—	—
E881	On or from ladders or scaffolding	—	—	—	—
E882	From or out of building or other structure	—	2	10	12
E883	Into hole or other opening	—	1	1	2
E884	From one level to another	2	3	4	9
E885	On same level from slipping, tripping or stumbling	—	—	—	—
E886	On same level from collision, pushing or shoving by or with another person	—	—	—	—
E888	Other and unspecified	—	2	2	4

Non-fatal falls

The numbers of children who seek hospital treatment following non-fatal falls are presented in Table 3. There are three points to be noted in relation to this table. First, the numbers it contains are estimates, derived from the home and leisure accident surveillance systems (HASS and LASS) run by the consumer safety unit of the Department of Trade and Industry.[2] In these systems, data on accidents are collected at a sample of hospitals throughout the UK by clerks who are placed in the accident and emergency departments. There are currently 22 hospitals at which home accident data are collected and 11 for so-called leisure accident data (a 'leisure' accident is defined as any accident that is not a home, road or occupational accident). The data collection systems are sufficiently well established to allow the samples based on these hospitals to be converted to national estimates. Secondly, these data relate to the UK, not England and Wales, unlike Tables 1 and 2. Thirdly, these are 1988 data, whereas the fatalities were for 1989.

It was noted above that the fatal falls make up less than 4% of the accidental child fatalities. By contrast, the non-fatal falls for which hospital treatment is sought comprise 45% of the home accidents and 50% of the leisure accidents.

Table 3.   Estimated numbers of non-fatal falls and all accidents, children aged 0–14 years, UK, 1988

Location	Non-fatal falls			All accidents
	Boys	Girls	Total	
Home	243,000	186,000	429,000	961,000
Leisure	398,000	255,000	653,000	1,308,000
Total	641,000	441,000	1,082,000	2,269,000

Falls on stairs and steps

A more extensive examination of Office of Population, Censuses and Surveys' records for ICD codes E880 and E884 for the period 1976–85 was undertaken as a part of a study of falls on stairs and steps.[3] For this ten-year period, these two E-codes represented about half of fatal falls among children under 15 years. Although they do not constitute a total picture of fatal falls, they reveal the link between age, and hence life-style and ability, and the type of fall experienced (Table 4).

Not surprisingly, all the fatal 'drops' were to children under two years, with the majority babies in the first year of life. Falls from furniture were also a characteristic fall among the very young. As children become older, the nature of falls they suffer and of those that cause death changes. The great majority of falls from play equipment and natural features (trees, cliffs, etc.) were suffered by children aged over five years, reflecting their change of range and activities. The exception to this bimodal split of falls by age is falls on stairs and steps. These are characterised by children in the age range 1–4 years, although there is an unexplained peak among children under six months old.

The purpose of this study was to examine falls on stairs and steps, so further details of these falls were obtained from coroners' records, a valuable and extensive, but under-utilised source of data (Table 5).[4] Within this subgroup were a further 15 cases in which a child was dropped, usually by the mother, 80% of which happened while the carrier was going down the stairs. The single case of a child being dropped who was older than 23 months was an eight-year-old mentally retarded boy who was being carried by his mother who fell from the second stair from the bottom of a flight. The child died from a fat embolus following a fractured femur.

Table 4. Nature of fatal falls (ICD codes E880 and E884) by age, England and Wales, 1976–85

Type of fall	Age group						Total	%
	0–5 mths	6–11 mths	12–23 mths	2–4 yrs	5–9 yrs	10–14 yrs		
Dropped	10	5	4	0	0	0	19	7.6
Fell from:								
furniture	5	13	12	9	3	3	45	18.1
pram, pushchair	2	2	0	0	2	1	7	2.8
play equipment	0	0	1	8	11	13	33	13.3
cliff, mountain, etc	0	0	0	0	10	29	39	15.7
tree	0	0	0	0	12	23	35	14.1
other	1	0	1	3	7	7	19	7.6
stairs, steps	9	4	16	16	4	3	52	20.9
Total	27	24	34	36	49	79	249	100

Table 5. Circumstances of fatal falls on stairs and steps by age group, England and Wales, 1976–85

Type of fall	Age group						Total	%
	0–5 mths	6–11 mths	12–23 mths	2–4 yrs	5–9 yrs	10–14 yrs		
Simple fall	0	0	8	8	0	1	17	52
Dropped while carrier going:								
up	1	1	0	0	0	0	2	6
down	7	2	2	0	1	0	12	36
not known	1	0	0	0	0	0	1	3
Sliding down	0	0	1	0	0	0	1	3
Total	9	3	11	8	1	1	33	100

It is interesting to examine these fatal stair falls further as this will
provide guidance on how to prevent them. Some facts about them are
that:

- in all 15 dropped child cases an adult was involved;
- in three of these drops, the mother's fall was caused by her fainting;
- six of the simple falls occurred with adults close at hand, actually accompa-
  nying the child in three cases, although always on the wrong side to prevent
  the fall (ahead when going up or behind when coming down), and in the
  other three cases the adult witnessed the fall;
- in the remaining 11 cases, there was an adult in the house.

Playground falls

The final topic is falls in playgrounds, in particular the role of the
surfacing material as a means of preventing or reducing the severity of
the resulting injuries. This is a subject about which there are misunder-
standings and too many unknowns. According to an analysis of LASS
data by Ball and King, there are about 42,000 playground accidents
requiring hospital attendance in the UK annually.[5] The Ball and King
paper, which follows from their earlier and more extensive examination of playground accident and injury prevention,[6] reveals that
there are about 2,000 admissions per year, half of them associated with
upper limb fractures and about 40% with actual or suspected head
injuries. Their analysis examined the accidents according to the
involvement of fixed play equipment. They found that about 8%
(some 3,300 accidents per year) were falls from such equipment,
resulting in either admission, a fracture or concussion—what they term
the serious injuries.

The area of contention is the role of impact absorbing surfacing to
meet the British Standard BS 7188 in playground safety as a whole.
This standard links the so-called critical height of equipment from
which children may fall to the energy absorbing requirements of the
surface. It allows a range of materials from sand and bark to rubber
tiles. The calculation of critical height for a given material depends on
the force experienced by a free-falling impactor and the time over
which this force lasts. The resulting number is associated with the
likelihood of an impact giving rise to permanent brain damage, and is
reasonably well founded having been developed over many years in
human tolerance research in the car industry.

Some commentators take Ball and King's findings to indicate that
the installation of such surfacing is not worthwhile, while others see
it as the universal panacea. In reality, its value is at some, so far
undefined, point between these extremes. It may make a contribution
along with good maintenance, well laid-out playgrounds, appropriate

and well installed equipment and supervision, but the extent of its contribution is still to be determined. Local authorities and others are asking if they need to spend millions of pounds to install impact absorbing surfacing to reduce injuries from falls, but the problem is that no one knows the answer. It is possible to hazard a guess at the annual number of head injuries throughout the UK that could be affected by such surfacing but, in reality, as the average length of inpatient stay is less than two days, it is unlikely that more than a handful, if any, of these are of a life-threatening nature. There has been no evaluation of the effects of the surfacing on injuries, an omission that must be corrected urgently.

Prevention of falls

There is a school of thought, largely North American-based, that believes that we should not talk about preventing falls but rather about preventing the injuries. It is difficult to argue against such a view, but if a countermeasure exists that allows the fall to be prevented (as is the case for some of the examples noted above) this seems to be an excellent way to prevent an injury.

Falls on stairs and playground falls allow the three classic prevention strategies to be illustrated:

- *education* of parents, especially by health visitors and general practitioners, must be used to reduce dropped child accidents on stairs;
- *engineering* and good design by architects, local authority housing departments, product manufacturers and many others can provide for easy installation of stairgates; in playgrounds, impact absorbing surfacing of proven effectiveness could reduce injury severity;
- *legislation* may be used to require local authorities and others to install such surfacing (while at the same time putting an onus on them to provide play facilities).

Conclusion

The means to prevent at least some of these accidents are readily available. The list of those who are in a position to advise on, implement or enforce such countermeasures is long and includes many specialties in the health professions. Those who have a professional role to maintain the good health of children and to treat their injuries are high on the list of those who have a clear responsibility and capability to set the prevention process in motion.

References

1. Office of Population, Censuses and Surveys. *Mortality statistics, accidents and violence. Series DH4, no. 15.* London: HMSO, 1991
2. Department of Trade and Industry. *Home and leisure accident research: 12th annual report home accident surveillance system, 1988 data.* London: Department of Trade and Industry, 1990
3. Nixon J, Jackson RH, Hayes HRM. *An analysis of childhood falls involving stairs and banisters.* London: Department of Trade and Industry, 1987
4. Levene S. Coroners' records of accidental deaths. *Arch Dis Child* 1991; **66**: 1239–41
5. Ball DJ, King KL. Playground injuries: a scientific appraisal of popular concerns. *J Roy Soc Health* 1991; **3**: 134–7
6. King KL, Ball DJ. *A holistic approach to accident and injury prevention in children's playgrounds.* London: London Scientific Services, 1989

5 | Preventing child traffic injuries

Robert Sunderland

Consultant Paediatrician, Selly Oak Hospital and Birmingham Accident Hospital

Introduction

The 400 million cars in the world cause 250,000 deaths per annum. Children as pedestrians and cyclists are among the most vulnerable.

All physical injuries are the consequence of energy transfers. In traffic injuries, the energy fluxes frequently result in serious or fatal damage. Of the 700 child deaths per annum from injury in England and Wales, 400 occur in traffic. The child victim is a pedestrian in half of them, and a cyclist and a vehicle occupant each in a quarter. In addition to the deaths, there are some 50,000 non-fatal child traffic injuries per annum in England and Wales, of which 10,000 are serious and 5–10% result in permanent disability. One child in 15 will be seriously injured in traffic before his 16th birthday.

Attempts to reduce this require attention to conflicting interests of vehicle manufacturers, road users and ministerial departments. Britain's overall road safety record is among the best in Europe because vehicle occupants have the lowest risk of mortality per 100,000 vehicle kilometres driven, but the number of child pedestrian injuries and fatalities per 100,000 child population is among the worst in Europe.

Incidents not accidents

Child traffic injuries have predictable and calculable risks. Boys are six times more vulnerable than girls, the peak age is 10–14 years, with the peak seasonal incidence during the early autumn months, especially in the evenings. Throughout the year, school entry and leaving are the most dangerous times and sites. Areas of social deprivation have much higher injury rates than areas of affluence because the environment, not the child, is accident-prone. Eighty-five per cent of child traffic fatalities occur in residential areas where traffic is light.

All children play. If there is crowded housing with no secure garden, the children will play in any available space including the street. If children are housed near areas of high traffic flow, it is statistically inevitable that children and vehicles will collide. Children congregate

at school gates at entry and leaving. In 1961 80% of children walked
to school, but in 1981 80% were driven to school. It is no longer
perceived safe for a child to walk to school, and the school gate is now a
high-risk zone for child traffic injuries.

Child traffic injuries occur principally in healthy children who were
expected to have led a productive life. The number of 'productive
years' lost in this way is greater than the number of such years lost
from all cancers, and as high as those lost from ischaemic heart disease
(because these diseases occur in older populations). Reducing child
traffic injuries must be a high priority in any public health strategy.

Child passenger injuries

Child passenger injuries can be reduced if seat-belts are worn at all
times, and if all drivers obey all motoring legislation. A child passenger
is ultimately at the mercy of drivers. Rear-facing reinforced bucket
seats for infants under one year are to be recommended, and appropriately adjusted three-point seat-belts for children over this age
should be used with correctly designed booster cushions where appropriate.

Child cycle injuries

Reducing child cycle injuries will require wearing of protective gar-
ments and appropriate parental control. Legislation forbids cycling on
pavements and motorways, but there is no other restriction regarding
age or competence before a child may wobble on to any highway.
Cycle injury rates are predictable by age, rising rapidly from 5 to 8
years, doubling by age 11, and doubling again by age 15. This is partly
related to children travelling further as they get older, but it may not
fully explain why the rise is exclusively among boy cyclists who have
six times as many cycling injuries as girls. While boys may manifest
greater interest in cycling, this difference may also reflect the more
adventurous behaviour of boys, who are at increased risk of all
accidents.

Injuries to the head have a far more serious outcome than injuries to
other parts of the body. Many cyclist head injuries occur when the
child strikes the ground rather than a vehicle. The severity of brain
injury is a consequence of energy flux, and could be effectively reduced
by the wearing of cycle helmets. Unfortunately, these are currently
perceived as 'sissy', but no sane cyclist would venture into modern
urban traffic without wearing one. Strategies are needed to make them
easily obtainable, affordable and fashionable.

European cycle injury rates are lower, partly because of a greater

awareness by drivers, who were or are also cyclists, of cyclists' instability, but also because of the widespread provision of bicycle lanes and
the segregation of motor vehicles from other road users. Britain has
much to learn about modifying the traffic environment to increase
safety for cyclists.

Child pedestrian injuries

Reduction of child pedestrian injuries is largely dependent upon adult
behaviour. Social and civil engineering may partly compensate for the
irresponsible behaviour of parents allowing immature children to
wander into a hostile environment unprotected. There is adequate
housing stock within most communities to allow families with young
children to be housed away from major traffic routes or preferably in
estates where through traffic is actively discouraged by road layout.

Similar social and civil engineering is available for the siting and
layout of school access. Excited children emerge from school gates with
little consideration of traffic danger. Their low stature makes them less
visible to motorists, and more difficult for them to see cars, especially if
there are parked vehicles. The school day commences at the time of
peak morning traffic flow, so starting the school day earlier would
reduce scholar vulnerability.

Forty seven per cent of all traffic injuries to children occur on
unclassified roads, a quarter of them in the street where the child lives.
On-street parking is the major contributory factor: one-third of child
injury victims say they were prevented from seeing on-coming traffic
by stationary cars, and 42% of drivers who have knocked down
children say they did not see the child until he emerged between the
parked cars immediately before impact. To reduce this type of injury,
traffic calming measures (to reduce speed or prevent through traffic),
re-arrangement of parking (to create open areas for play where
children are visible), and improvement of safe off-street play areas will
be needed.

The analysis of fatal child pedestrian injuries identifies several
contributory factors:

- the child's unpredictable behaviour (the major cause), 84%;
- the environment, 47%; and
- reckless behaviour of the driver, 12% (8% resulting in prosecution).

Children are both the victims and the cause of most pedestrian
accidents, but are the least equipped to take preventive or avoiding
action. They lack the developmental skills because of their vulnerability and immaturity. Time and resources spent on education on
road safety may be inappropriate if the child is developmentally

incapable of coping safely with modern traffic. It is impossible to expect children to modify playing behaviour until childishness matures out of them. Preventive measures must also target other factors, including the driver and the environments since adults often have unrealistic expectations of children's abilities and behaviour.

Accident-prone drivers

There is an over-representation of young males among the drivers involved in serious child traffic injuries. These men have no recent experience of children, and are the most unrealistic in their expectation of a child's abilities. They need, both psychologically and biologically, to demonstrate their potency. Those drivers least likely to modify speed or road position do this posturing in neighbourhoods where children live but where they are not always visible or expected. It is idealistic, but unrealistic to expect these young males to alter such behaviour. Eighty-five per cent of drivers who fail a breath test are males, usually aged 25–45 years. Alcohol-influenced driving is not a major component in child incidents; however, the continued behaviour of these drivers, despite legislation, advertising and stigmatisation, suggests that attempts to modify other drivers' behaviour by education or legislation may founder.

Accident-prone environments

The most effective strategy to reduce child traffic injuries is traffic calming by directed and planned neighbourhood engineering. Such modifications to the environment are both successful and cost-effective. Where planned carefully and appropriately applied, there are continued long-term improvements in environmental safety. If applied rashly, without adequate consideration of the whole neighbourhood, a traffic calming strategy may simply lead to run-off of traffic from a main route into residential areas, with a creation of 'rat runs' which increase the danger to pedestrians throughout the surrounding area.

Separation of children and vehicles by the widespread use of pedestrianised areas in European cities has made these cities pleasant to visit, and safer for both adults and children. Germany has higher car ownership than Britain, yet the level of child pedestrian injuries is much lower. This is because German children have a much higher status in their society than British children have here, there is much higher adult awareness of child behaviour, and traffic calming measures, bicycle lanes and pedestrianised areas are widespread. The '20 plus' statistical mnemonic contains proof that traffic calming is effective and necessary (Table 1).

Table 1.   The '20 plus' mnemonic for traffic calming measures

Speed of traffic (mph)	No. child vehicle collisions resulting in death
20	5% (1 in 20)
30	50% (20 + 30)
40	90% (20 + 30 + 40)

Changing the agenda

Reducing child traffic injuries will require considerable exchequer resources, and therefore considerable political will. The compulsory wearing of seat-belts was resisted by British politicians on the grounds that it infringed individual freedom. One of the factors that influenced the introduction of seat-belt legislation was when increasing ortho-paedic waiting lists reached political awareness—these waiting lists could never be reduced as long as the results of weekend traffic collisions continued to block beds. By changing the political agenda, appropriate legislation was introduced, with a subsequent reduction in vehicle occupant injuries.

The agenda may also change if the cost to society of ignoring the problem becomes known. In 1984, child injuries consumed £10 of health service resources per resident child. Thus, a city with one million children expended £10 million on the first-aid care of its injured children. Long-term costs are geometrically higher: 3% of child traffic victims die, 3% are severely disabled, and 7% have some residual permanent handicap. In fact, child traffic injuries remove more healthy lives than war or terrorism. More Americans die on their roads each year than were killed in the whole of the Vietnam War, and in Northern Ireland, four people die on the roads for every death by bomb or bullet.

Preventive strategies

Preventive strategies can be grouped into three categories:

- innovation;
- education; and
- legislation.

Innovative engineering is by far the most cost-effective of these, with revenue savings continuing into the future.

The increasing volumes of traffic within urban centres, largely due to the increasing use of private cars, and leading to near thrombosis of some cities, have been associated with a deterioration of the urban environment and may be one factor in the unexplained increase of childhood illnesses. The polluting effects of vehicle exhausts will ultimately result in public action to preserve the environment.

In Japan it is now necessary to show proof of ownership of a parking space before a vehicle may be purchased. Californians (long the advocates of individual freedom) have demanded tax increases to fund development of public transport systems. Across Europe, quality of life is considered at least equal to that of self determination, with consequent improvement in the urban environment.

Solzhenitsyn, writing from the Gulag, considered that the car was the ultimate icon of individual liberty because of the freedom of movement it represents—but ultimate freedom leads only to tyranny, and community action addressing a much wider agenda may be needed to restrict and control the hazard which the motor car represents to modern life.

The role of the medical profession

Doctors have not always been vociferous in publicising the threat that vehicles (especially the motor car) represent to modern society, which may be misinterpreted as a manifestation of self interest. Professions misrepresent themselves as a conspiracy against the laity by active disinterest in prevention. Physicians could refute such charges by their public statements about reducing diseases caused by smoking, alcohol, inappropriate diet, the environment, and now childhood accidents. However, the doggerel should be borne in mind:

> It was a dangerous cliff, as they freely confessed
> but to walk near its edge was so pleasant
> that over its terrible edge there had slipped
> a duke and full many a peasant.
> So the people said 'something will have to be done',
> but their projects did not at all tally:
> Some said put a hedge around the edge of the cliff;
> the doctor put an ambulance down in the valley.

(Anon)

Further reading

1. Lawson S. *Accidents to young pedestrians: distributions, circumstances, consequences and scope for countermeasures*. London: Automobile Association Foundation for Road Safety Research and Birmingham City Council, 1990
2. Jackson RH. Hazards to children in traffic. *Arch Dis Child* 1978; **53**: 807–13
3. Jackson RH, ed. *Children, the environment and accidents*. Tunbridge Wells: Pitman Medical, 1977

6 | Preventing burn and scald accidents in children

Roger Cudmore

Consultant Paediatric Surgeon, Alder Hey Children's Hospital, Liverpool

Introduction

She was not unintelligent—indeed, she had watched the previous Sunday's TV programme on burns and scalds, which was part of the *Play it safe* series, introduced by Jimmy Savile at the peak viewing time of 6.15 p.m. The programme on scalds and burns was particularly well done because it was filmed from below, showing how a toddler's world was viewed from that upward direction.

Two days later she found herself in a children's burns unit 100 miles from home with her child who had climbed into a bath of hot water and been severely scalded. On talking to her, it was clear that she remembered the TV programme. She said that she had found it fascinating, and had particularly noted how it had been filmed from below, which she thought was very good and thought-provoking. The doctor discussed the programme content with her and asked how much she remembered about what had been said in relation to bath water. She recalled it had been said that not only should children be well supervised at bath time but that it was vital to put the cold water in first. When asked if she had done that, she replied, 'Oh, no—I put the hot in first as I always do'.

This true story illustrates the difficulty of preventing skin damage which, so far as toddlers are concerned, rarely kills—there have been only two scald deaths in 20 years at Alder Hey—but which causes permanent scarring of the child's body and of the parent's psyche. After 20 years of supervising a children's burns unit I have come to wonder what can be done to prevent a disease which seems to defy eradication.

What needs to be done?

First, the size of the problem has to be determined. Here, we are bedevilled by a plethora of statistics, although all agree that this is a major public health problem. About 120 children a year are admitted to our unit suffering from scalds, of whom half will need a skin graft. At least twice as many are seen in casualty with smaller areas of injury which do not merit admission. These statistics have not changed over the years.

On the other hand, there is a marked decrease in burns compared with 20 years ago when night-dress and clothing burns were more common. With legislation on flammable materials and the increase in centrally-heated homes, true flame burns are now rare, but it is still possible to buy flammable materials on market stalls. I believe that everything possible has probably been done in relation to burn prevention, although young and older children still set themselves alight by playing with matches or electric power lines.

It is self-evident that the tragic deaths from house conflagrations can be avoided only by the removal of flammable materials from homes and public meeting-places. The effect of the recent campaign to install smoke detectors in houses awaits assessment.

Can the true incidence be estimated?

The Hospital Inpatient Enquiry (HIE) enquiry in 1981 estimated that a total of 4,460 children in the 0–4 age group were discharged or died from burns and scalds each year and 1,050 in the 5–14 age group.[1] If our figure of about 120 children per year admitted with damage greater than 10% or in areas difficult to manage is average for burns units throughout Great Britain, there is currently an average of 3,900 admissions a year nationwide for scalds. This would suggest that the incidence has not changed much since 1981.

The Child Accident Prevention Trust (CAPT) would agree with this,[2] saying that:

> from the little that has been written about scald injuries it would appear that they have not declined . . . the pattern in terms of the hazards posed by cups, saucepans, teapots and kettles remains depressingly similar to that identified by Colebrook in 1949.[3]

I would only add that compared with 40 years ago (*vide supra*), deaths are now—or should be—very rare.

If this is a major public health problem, as I believe it is, how should it be tackled? Do we wish and care enough to tackle it?

Education, engineering and enforcement
Education

The value of education in producing a direct reduction in the number of childhood accidents is probably limited, in that its immediate effect is short-term and the recommended actions soon forgotten.

Exhortations such as 'always put cold water in the bath before putting in the hot' are of little use. Indeed, it has been pointed out that the effectiveness of accident prevention measures varies inversely with the frequency with which the action has to be carried out. Actions cannot 'always or never' be carried out. It is more effective to carry out one preventive action, for example, to get the thermostat right, or buy a safer design of kettle. Most effective of all is to build in safety at the design stage so that no action is needed; for example, to ban unbarred electric fires or withdraw all but curly-flexed kettles. The use of coiled kettles or sprung electric flexes is supported, and education or advertising to promote their use should be more widely used. In order to reduce the spillage of water, the wider use of spout-filled kettles is also supported.

Education must have a role in influencing behaviour, although it may take a generation of continuing education to produce a permanent change. Perhaps the most important aspect of education is to create awareness of a problem and an opinion such that safe design and safety measures become acceptable, desirable and useful. For example, if the temperature of tap-water is controlled thermostatically, the temperature should be set at a maximum of 54°C (130°F). The use of thermostatically controlled mixer taps is to be encouraged. A recent questionnaire survey of the parents of the last 25 admissions to our unit which asked, among other things, how they thought the injury could have been prevented, had a 60% response. Most of the parents, although sad about the damage caused, did not think at the time that much could have been done to prevent their child's accident. They had not thought their child would move so quickly to interact with the hot liquid. Interestingly, they had all used cold water to pour on the wound to reduce the heat, but not all of them did so with the clothing still in place, so time was lost in cooling the area.

In 1980, Alyson Learmouth, in a study of thermal injuries in Bradford, wrote:

> Health education appears to have little effect in changing dangerous behaviour patterns. In addition, some accidents may be attributable simply to poor living conditions.[4]

Engineering

The importance of engineering and design is self-evident and has been widely considered in relation to the macro-environment of town planning, but the micro-environment of the home is even more important, given that most accidents happen at home. Safety aspects should be pursued through publicity and acceptance of the guidelines on *Child safety and housing*, produced by CAPT.[5]

Product design has to be consistently monitored from the safety point of view. Consumer associations are vital in criticising, condemning and recommending, but their views have to be transmitted nationwide and not just to *Guardian* readers. Why, for example, put electrical sockets low down where they are most easily available to inquisitive hands?

Enforcement

How can safety be enforced? We have been involved with Granada TV in producing teaching films on accidents and their prevention to be shown to teenagers, many of whom would soon leave school and become parents themselves—but is this sufficient? Do they remember what they have been shown? The survey mentioned above would suggest not. Should there be a penal code?

Conclusions

There is scope for more safety education to be given by health professionals, with health visitors having a special role. It should be given greater emphasis in the school curriculum. The availability of fire officers to support fire safety teaching should be more widely publicised among education authorities.*

The education of those responsible for policy relating to and for the design of our physical, social and economic environments is of paramount importance in reducing burn and scald accidents.

This chapter is the distillation of experience in a designated children's unit, of which sadly there are few in the country.

Acknowledgement

My thanks go to the unswerving loyalty and care of Sister Hodge and her staff, who have cared so lovingly for so many children.

References

1. Department of Health and Social Security. *Hospital Inpatient Enquiry no. 18*. London: HMSO, 1983
2. Child Accident Prevention Trust. *Burn and scald accidents to children*. London: Bedford Square Press. 1985
3. Colebrook L, Colebrook V. The prevention of burns and scalds. *Lancet* 1949; **ii**: 181–8
4. Learmouth A. *Factors in child burn and scald accidents: a review of the literature*. Bradford: University of Bradford, 1980
5. Child Accident Prevention Trust. *Child safety and housing*. London: Bedford Square Press, 1985

---

* *Since writing this, the BBC has shown another series of safety programmes hosted by Anneka Rice.*

7 | Drowning and near-drowning in children

Jo Sibert

Department of Community Child Health, University of Wales College of Medicine, Community Health Unit, Lansdowne Hospital, Cardiff, Wales

Alison Kemp

Senior Registrar, University of Wales College of Medicine, Community Health Unit, Lansdowne Hospital, Cardiff, Wales

Introduction

Drowning and near-drowning in children present challenging problems, both in the assessment and treatment of the nearly-drowned child and in the prevention of the incident. Drowning is a considerable public health problem in children in warm advanced countries.[1,2] Indeed, much of the research on drowning and near-drowning in childhood has been performed in the USA and Australia. In Britain, drowning in children has been less researched than in those water-orientated societies. However, we have recently been fortunate to have the use of the British Paediatric Surveillance Unit to perform an integrated study of drowning and near drowning in children in the UK in 1988 and 1989.[3,4]

How many children drown?

Drowning is the third most common cause of accidental death in children in the UK. In 1988–89, 306 children had confirmed submersion incidents: 149 died and 157 survived after near-drowning, 10 of whom sustained severe neurological deficit.[3] Most of the children were under five years of age. Drowning is an unusual accident, however, and, unlike most other accidents, an infrequent cause of presentation to the accident and emergency department. Many near-drowning cases who are admitted to hospital are seriously ill and have to be admitted to the intensive care unit (ICU).

Many more boys drown than girls, which reflects the different behaviour patterns of boys. There are also heavy social-class gradients, with disadvantaged children more likely to drown. One mode of drowning that does not follow this pattern is death in private swimming pools.

43

The annual incidence in England and Wales of submersion accidents for children under 15 years of age is 1.5 per 100,000, with a mortality rate of 0.7 per 100,000. Boys under five have the highest incidence of submersion (3.6 per 100,000).[4] In the USA, drowning death rates are as high as 1 per 8,000 boys aged 2–3 years in Los Angeles County,[2] and in Australia drowning is the most common cause of death for children between one and five years.[5]

Where do children drown?

Children drown wherever there is water (Table 1). Each age group in childhood is associated with drowning in a particular site:

- Babies: bath drownings.
- Toddlers: garden ponds and domestic swimming pools.
- Older children: open water, and municipal and private swimming pools.

Table 1. Cases of drowning in children under 15 years of age in the UK 1988–9 grouped according to site of incident (141 notified in 1988, 165 in 1989) (numbers in brackets are survivors who sustained severe neurological handicap)

	Survivors near drowning	Drowning deaths	Total	Mean age
Bath	19 (1)	25	44	1 y 2 m
Garden pond	48 (4)	11	59	1 y 10 m
Domestic pool	15 (2)	18	33	2 y 4 m
Private pool	10	8	18	5 y 9 m
River/canal/lake	17 (2)	56	73	6 y 10 m
Public pool	30 (1)	2	32	7 y
Sea	9	20	29	7 y 10 m
Other	9	9	18	4 y 2 m
Total	157 (10)	149	306	

y = years; m = months

Why do children drown?

Supervision of children is vital if they have access to water. In 86% of drowning incidents in the UK study the children were unsupervised. The importance of supervision is also shown by the very few children who die from drowning in municipal swimming pools where there is clear supervision under the Health and Safety at Work Act. A lack of swimming ability may be a factor in drowning, but most of the children in the study were too young to swim. A very few younger children are deliberately drowned, usually in the bath.

What is the outlook for the near-drowned child?

In the British study, 31 of 64 children unconscious on admission had normally reactive pupils, and all but three (all of whom had severe pre-existing neurological disease and secondary drowning complications) made a full recovery.[3] Of the 33 patients with fixed dilated pupils on admission, ten made a full recovery, 13 died and ten sustained severe neurological deficit in the form of a spastic quadriplegia with profound learning difficulties.

Spontaneous respiratory effort on admission was associated with normal survival. Pupils that remained dilated after six hours' admission and fits continuing 24 hours after admission predicted poor outcome.

Three studies in the USA have shown that fixed dilated pupils and coma after severe submersion incidents predict those children who will die or have neurological deficit.[6-8] These studies may relate to children drowning in the relatively warm pools in the USA. In contrast, it was found in the UK that some children survive normally after severe submersion incidents despite being admitted to hospital unconscious with fixed dilated pupils. Patients with impaired levels of consciousness with reactive pupils have a good prognosis as do the children with respiratory effort on admission.

Why should some patients, apparently dead on admission with fixed dilated pupils, survive normally?

It has been suggested that man has a vestigial diving reflex, which is more marked in children and is exaggerated by cold and fear. This may explain why some children, apparently dead on admission and with fixed dilated pupils, survive normally after a long period of immersion. The ability of diving mammals to remain under water, sometimes for up to 30 minutes, is due to this reflex, in which the peripheral circulation is shut down, with a profound bradycardia and with the brain achieving most of its circulation. Recent work suggests that the diving reflex is not active in humans.[9]

Harries has suggested that submersion hypothermia is the reason some people survive prolonged periods under water, with the rapid fall in body temperature on immersion in cold water exerting a protective cranial hypothermia before the circulation falls.[10] Orlowski has used the term 'ice water' drowning rather than 'cold water' drowning, because a review of the world's medical literature revealed that all the cases with a good outcome after prolonged immersion occurred in water at a temperature of 10°C or less.[11] This suggests also that it is the hypothermia that is protective, with this effect being more pronounced in children than in adults because children have a higher surface area to body weight ratio, and therefore cool more rapidly. Most outdoor drownings in the UK are in water temperatures of less than 20°C, and submersion hypothermia may well play an important part in normal recovery. All four of the children in our series with fixed dilated pupils and no respiratory effort on admission to hospital who survived normally had a temperature less than 32°C, and three were profoundly hypothermic.

How should the near-drowned child be treated?

Waterside resuscitation of the near-drowned child is important, and cardiopulmonary resuscitation should be started as soon as possible after the child has been taken from the water. As much water as possible should first be cleared from the airways, and further heat loss prevented.

If the child is conscious on admission to hospital, a cautious approach should be taken because some children may develop secondary respiratory complications, such as aspiration pneumonitis and secondary drowning.

If the child is unconscious on admission, he should be admitted to the ICU, and in most cases be electively ventilated and rewarmed slowly. Some children who come to hospital unconscious with fixed dilated pupils survive normally, so resuscitation should not be abandoned until the child is rewarmed. Although fixed dilated pupils on admission is not a reliable predictor of outcome for the child after a serious submersion incident, the pupillary reflex is a neurological sign unaffected by the drugs used in the electively ventilated paralysed patient, and it becomes a useful indicator of outcome during this form of treatment. All patients in the study who made a full recovery had normal sustained pupil reactivity within six hours of cardiopulmonary resuscitation. If fixed dilated pupils persist after six hours and the child has been rewarmed, brain death criteria should be sought.

Convulsions limited to the first 24 hours carry no prognostic significance. Prolonged, poorly controlled fits beyond the first day of hospitalisation are associated with neurological deficit.

How can children be prevented from drowning?

Children do not drown in the bath or garden ponds while supervised.

Although environmental change is more effective than education in accident prevention,[12] there is evidence that health visitors can get families to make their home safer.[13] Mothers should therefore be told about the dangers of drowning in baths, garden ponds and other receptacles as part of a child surveillance programme. Families should be discouraged from having unprotected ornamental ponds in their gardens. Ponds could be fenced, particularly in parks and garden centres. The use of a sturdy grid just under the water surface may prove an effective safety feature. Modification of the Building Act 1984 could be considered in the future to bring safety of garden ponds under the building regulations.

Domestic swimming pools were shown to be a significant problem in England and Wales in 1982,[14] and regrettably this continues. Far fewer children are exposed to domestic pools than to public pools where the mortality rate is remarkably low. Pool covers are involved in many of the accidents in domestic pools. Covers are required to prevent heat loss and reduce pool debris, but they are often opaque, hug the water surface and are non-weight bearing.

There is good evidence from Australia,[15,16] New Zealand[17] and the USA[18] that fencing 1.5 m high, including specially designed self-locking gates can prevent drowning in domestic pools. Fencing has been introduced by regulation in parts of these countries. Any such legislation is still awaited in the UK.

It is likely that the high level of supervision insisted on by the Code of Practice on Safety in Swimming Pools, introduced under the Health and Safety at Work Act 1974,[19] is responsible for the low mortality in public pools.[20] More children die in private pools than in public pools, suggesting that safety standards are not as high in the former. Environmental health officers recently highlighted their concerns regarding the level of supervision in these pools.[21]

It is good sense to believe that teaching children to swim would prevent some of these accidents. However, it was not possible to confirm this in our study because of the young age of most of the children. In any case, swimming proficiency gained in a heated pool is likely to be considerably less effective in the cold open waters of Great Britain.[2] Water safety advice should be included when teaching children to swim and in the National Curriculum.

In Australia, life-guards are present on all major beaches.[22] The Royal Life Saving Society, UK-survey of 51 British beaches judged over half to have inadequate provisions for beach safety, and suggested safety recommendations which outline clear life-guard initiatives.[23] These should be extended to in-shore areas advertised for sport and recreation. If this is not possible, local councils should consider restricting swimming access. There should be considerable caution by youth organisations in having organised swimming parties at lakes and rivers.

Proposed safety agenda

The introduction in the UK of the following safety agenda could prevent many drowning incidents.

General:

- Maintain an on-going national system of collecting information on drowning deaths.

Bath:

- Use child surveillance programmes to inform parents of dangers.

Garden pond:

- Encourage fencing or draining of garden ponds.
- Evaluate safety grids.
- Consider placing safety requirements under building regulations.
- Use child surveillance programmes to inform parents of dangers.

Public pool:

- Maintain high level of surveillance under the Health and Safety at Work Act 1974.

Private pool:

- Extend high level of surveillance to these pools.

Domestic pool:

- Install fences (1.5 m) and self-locking gates around pools, if necessary by legislation.
- Review pool cover design.
- Keep a register of pools.

Open water:

- Supervise or restrict access for swimming in lakes and rivers.
- Youth organisations not to organise swimming parties in lakes and rivers.
- Extend life-guard control to major beaches.
- Include water safety in the National Curriculum and in swimming programmes.
- Life-jackets and buoyancy aids to be worn in boats and crafts.

References

1. Nixon J, Pearn J, Wilkey I, Corcoran A. A fifteen year study of child drowning. *Accid Anal Prev* 1986; **18**: 199–203
2. O'Carroll PW, Alkon E, Weiss B. Drowning mortality in Los Angeles County 1976 to 1984. *JAMA* 1988; **260**: 380–3
3. Kemp AM, Sibert JR. Outcome for children who nearly drown: a British Isles study. *Br Med J* 1991; **302**: 931–3
4. Kemp AM, Sibert JR. Drowning and near drowning in children in the United Kingdom: lessons for prevention. *Br Med J* 1992; **304**: 1143–6
5. Pearn J, Nixon J. Swiming pool immersion incidents. *Med J Aust* 1977; **1**: 432–7
6. Peterson B. Morbidity of childhood near drowning. *Pediatrics* 1977; **59**: 364–70
7. Modell JH, Graves SA, Ketover A. Clinical course of 91 consecutive near drowning victims. *Chest* 1976; **70**: 231–8
8. Frates RC. Analysis of predictive factors in the assessment of warm water near drowning in children. *Am J Dis Child 1981;* **135**: 1006–8
9. Ramey CA, Ramey DN, Hayward JS. Dive response of children in relation to cold water drowning. *J Appl Physiol* 1987; **63**: 665–8
10. Harries M. Drowning and near drowning. *Br Med J* 1986; **293**: 123–4
11. Orlowski JP. Drowning, near drowning and ice water drowning. *JAMA* 1988; **260**:390–1
12. Sibert JR. Accidents to children: the doctor's role. Education or environmental change. *Arch Dis Child* 1991; **66**: 890–4
13. Colver AF, Hutchinson PJ, Judson EC. Promoting children's home safety. *Br Med J* 1982; **285**: 1177–80
14. Barry W, Little TM, Sibert JR. Childhood drownings in private swimming pools—an avoidable cause of death. *Br Med J* 1982; **285**: 542–3
15. Pearn JH, Nixon J. Are swimming pools becoming more dangerous? *Med J Aust* 1977; **2**: 702–4
16. Milliner N, Pearn J, Guard R. Will fenced pools save lives? *Med J Aust* 1980; **2**: 510–1
17. Langley J. Fencing of private swimming pools in New Zealand. *Community Health Stud* 1983; **7**: 285–9
18. Orlowski JP. It's time for pediatricians to 'rally round the pool fence'. *Pediatrics* 1989; **83**: 1065–6
19. *Health and Safety at Work Act 1974*. London: HMSO, 1974
20. *Safety in swimming pools*. London: The Sports Council, 1988
21. Heyward K, Avery J. *Health and safety standards of swimming pools enforced by local authorities*. London: Institute of Environmental Health Officers, 1991
22. Patrick M, Bint M, Pearn J. Saltwater drowning and near drowning accidents involving children. *Med J Aust* 1979; **1**: 61–4
23. Beach safety. *Holiday Which?* 1991; 8 January: 30–3
24. *Beach safety press pack*. London: Royal Life Saving Society, UK, 1990

8 | Paediatric accident and emergency medicine: a challenge to paediatricians

John Glasgow*

*Reader, Department of Child Health, The Queen's University of Belfast;
Consultant Paediatrician, Accident and Emergency Department, Royal
Belfast Hospital for Sick Children*

Andrew Glasgow

Medical Student

Introduction

With the establishment of a subspeciality group, the British Paediatric
Accident and Emergency Group, within the framework of the British
Paediatric Association, accident and emergency (A & E) paediatrics is
growing up. Together with the British Association for Accident and
Emergency Medicine, there are now professional associations concerned with the practice of A & E medicine at all ages. Although it has
been stated that approximately two million children are seen annually
in A & E departments,[1] more recently this figure has been put at
greater than three million,[2] of whom at least 1.5 million are new
attenders. The majority of these are managed in general, largely adult-
orientated departments. In the British Isles only four paediatricians
have a full-time commitment to A & E paediatrics, with eight others
working part-time.

This chapter will survey current practice, outline the nature and
range of A & E work, as assessed in a recent clinical audit study using a
novel system of computerised A & E records, and suggest practical
ways in which paediatricians might respond, with the aim of promoting development of this field, which Hugh Jackson has called 'the
Cinderella of the services for children'.[1]

Accident and emergency philosophy and activities

Although the A & E department is geographically part of hospital

* Correspondence to: J. F. T. Glasgow, Department of Child Health, The Queen's
University of Belfast, Institute of Clinical Science, Grosvenor Road, Belfast BT12 6BJ,
Northern Ireland.

medicine, operationally it appears to be more akin to the community health service. While A & E doctors enjoy immediate access to services such as radiology and orthopaedics, the laboratories and high-dependency care, most patients do not need them. Because of the accessibility of an A & E department, self-referral and unbooked general practitioner (GP) referrals are common. This means that the nature and range of clinical conditions mirror those current in the community. The open-door policy makes for close professional relationships with GPs and community child health services, as well as for monitoring of childhood accidents and indices of local child health. This is facilitated by liaison health visiting. Moreover, the process of clinical decision making and the factors which influence it closely resemble those pertaining to general practice.[3]

A & E departments probably have a broader range of activities than is generally appreciated. Apart from the varied tasks of dealing with illness, injury and poisoning, there is the need to provide immediate advice to and support of the primary care team. As long ago as 1959, the Platt Report recognised that A & E staff must:

> co-operate in the researches being carried out into the best methods of preventing road accidents[4]

—to which we would add that they should also play a central role in district injury (accident) prevention initatives.

Other activities may be less obvious (Table 1). Underlying all these activities is the principle that, within the bounds of good clinical practice, children should be kept out of and away from hospital.[5] For those who do become statistics, it is essential to capture and store core data.

Table 1. Activities of an accident and emergency department

---

1. Management of childhood illness, injury and poisoning.
2. Resuscitation of the critically ill and injured.
3. High index of suspicion for detection of child abuse.
4. Close support of and liaison with community child health and primary care.
5. Accident prevention.
6. Confirmation of death in those apparently dead on arrival; and support and comfort of bereaved relatives.
7. Supplementation of local immunisation practice, and monitoring of this and other indices of local child health and morbidity.
8. Discouragement of inappropriate self-referral, unnecessary admission to hospital, etc.
9. Teaching, audit, research.

Information technology

An appropriate system

Large numbers of patients are seen per unit time (a large children's department sees more than 40,000 new patients annually), so a computerised system is essential for the recording, storage and retrieval of clinical records. This not only enhances clinical management but also facilitates audit and research. A number of information technology systems have been developed for use in A & E departments (e.g. CAER, SMS, PAS), but these have been designed for the greater numbers of patients seen in largely adult departments, are relatively complex and tend to be expensive to purchase and operate.

Our requirements were for a software package which would be 'user-friendly', could be operated by existing clerical staff (and therefore had no additional revenue consequences), and employed a fast microprocessor so that visual display unit response time would be extremely brief. A Xenix operating system and an Informix database were selected, linked to a Uniplex word-processing package to facilitate secretarial work. Hardware consists of an Olivetti XP5 computer which has an 80386 microprocessor, a 130-megabyte (MB) hard disk and a 60-MB tape streamer to carry out backup. An important specification was that the system should interface with other current information technology developments, such as radiology. The total cost (in 1990) was about £15,000.*

The clinical record

The clinical record sheet is relatively simple, but it more than meets the Körner requirements (Fig. 1). The upper panel (1) contains basic information about the patient and family doctor, the precise day and time of attendance and name of the child health clinic or school. In the central panel (2), the doctor's clinical notes, treatment, etc. are written, together with the time at which the consultation began. In the bottom panel (3) are recorded the diagnoses (up to three are accepted), disposal details and a mandatory field stating whether, according to previously agreed criteria, the daily liaison health visitor should be informed. Data contained in panels (1) and (3) are entered in the database. A simplified diagnostic coding system (of 366 codes) has been developed, bearing in mind the diagnostic limitations in an A & E department given the relative inexperience of medical staff and inevitable time pressure.

---

* Further details may be obtained from Sherwood Systems Ltd, The Midland Building, Whitla Street, Belfast BT15 1JP.

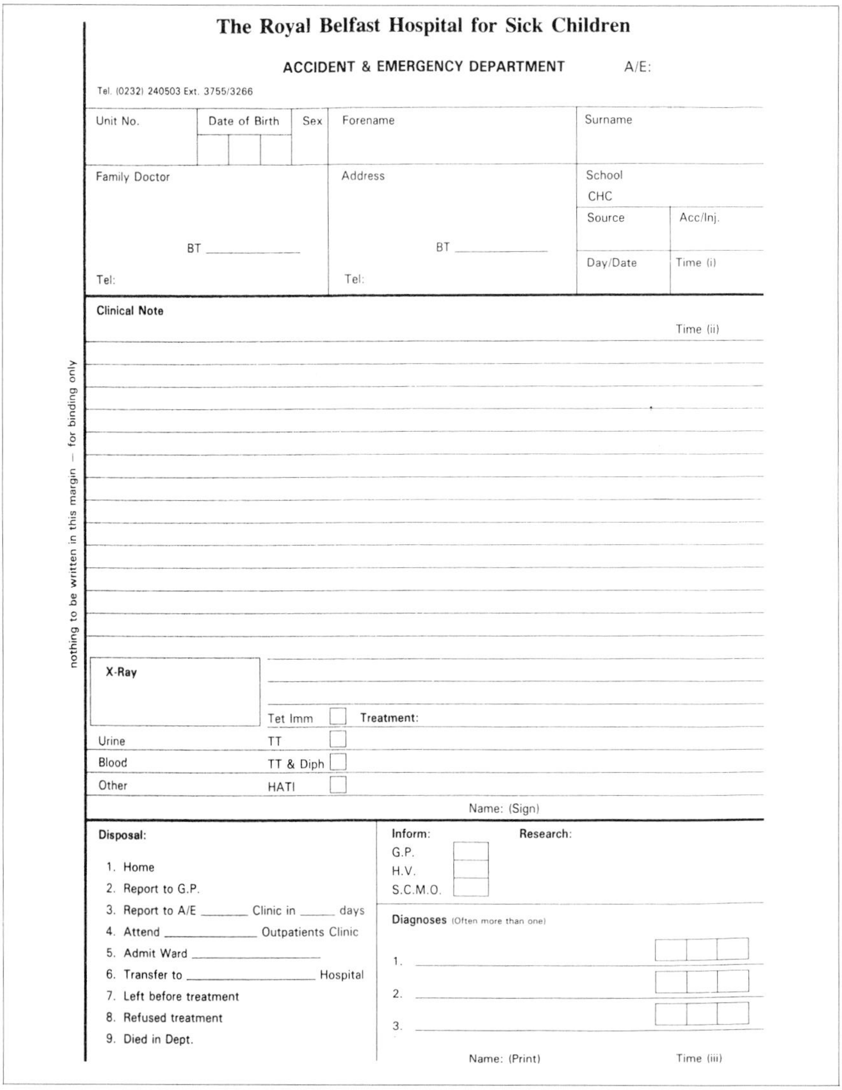

The Royal Belfast Hospital for Sick Children

ACCIDENT & EMERGENCY DEPARTMENT   A/E:

Tel. (0232) 240503 Ext. 3755/3266

Unit No.	Date of Birth	Sex	Forename		Surname	

Family Doctor		Address		School		
				CHC		
				Source	Acc/Inj.	
BT _____		BT _____		Day/Date	Time (i)	
Tel:		Tel:				

Clinical Note

Time (ii)

nothing to be written in this margin – for binding only

X-Ray

	Tet Imm ☐	Treatment:
Urine	TT ☐	
Blood	TT & Diph ☐	
Other	HATI ☐	

Name: (Sign)

Disposal:

1. Home
2. Report to G.P.
3. Report to A/E _____ Clinic in _____ days
4. Attend _____ Outpatients Clinic
5. Admit Ward _____
6. Transfer to _____ Hospital
7. Left before treatment
8. Refused treatment
9. Died in Dept.

Inform: Research:
G.P. ☐
H.V. ☐
S.C.M.O. ☐

Diagnoses (Often more than one)

1. _____
2. _____
3. _____

Name: (Print)   Time (iii)

Fig. 1. *The clinical record sheet, the three parts of which relate to (1) the patient, the general practitioner and the timing of the attendance; (2) the clinical notes; and (3) the diagnosis and disposal details.*

Operation of the system

Each new *attendance* (incident-based) is assigned a unique number, and at each subsequent *new* attendance the hard copy of the patient's previous record is retrieved and attached to that being generated. The record sheet is printed in triplicate in the form of continuous stationery, one copy is to be used as a radiology request, one for the family doctor,[6] and one copy filed. Should review be required, a continuation page is appended, although this is not computerised.

Audit materials and methods

The type and range of medical and surgical conditions dealt with are considered to be not unrepresentative of A & E work generally. The department is situated in a 172-bed teaching hospital within a socially disadvantaged, inner-city health district with particular problems of unemployment, and with over-representation of social classes IV–V and single-parent families. The child population (up to the 13th birthday) served is about 70,000, some 35% of whom are seen annually.[7] This is considerably higher than current estimates (20–25%) of the child population who attend an A & E department each year.[8]

Entry of patient information began in August 1990, and after 12 months the system contained 24,648 new attendance records. Audit was carried out (by A.J.G.) on a 5.2% random sample comprising 1,282 records. The hard copy of all but ten (which could not be located) was retrieved, carefully checked, errors corrected, and missing information entered where this could be inferred from the clinical notes. All the data in panels (1) and (3) were then transcribed onto Epi Info version 5 for statistical analysis.[9] Information on treatment had to be extracted manually and entered in the database. If it had been the intention to audit reviews, data would also have required extraction from the continuation records.

Audit results

Although A & E work can be individually unpredictable, certain characteristic diurnal and seasonal trends are apparent. More than 95% of patients are usually seen between the hours of 9 am and 9 pm, grouped in two clusters at approximately 12 noon and 6 pm. Less than 5% attend between midnight and 9 am. Various factors influence attendance and admission, some of which will be discussed in this chapter. An obvious factor is the type and degree of illness, but others, such as home circumstances, mother's competence or the ability and experience of junior medical staff, are more complex.[10]

Age

The audit confirmed that age is a major determinant. Infants constituted almost one-fifth (18%) of new attendances. With each additional year of age, the proportion in the sample tended to decrease. More than half (53%) were less than four years of age and 65% less than seven.

Sex

Boys were more likely to attend at all ages (M:F ratio, 1.38). A similar ratio (1.37) has been reported for children aged 0–14 years of age in three similar, inner London wards.[11] Infants in our study had a higher ratio (1.7).

Referral source

The open-door policy has the obvious disadvantage that many patients refer themselves (77% in this study), almost five times those referred by family doctors (16%). Those brought in by emergency ambulance accounted for 4.8% (see below).

Diagnosis

All of those with extant records had a diagnosis recorded, 10.5% had a second, and 1.2% a third. The commoner groups of diagnoses are shown in Table 2, both for the sample as a whole and for the 241 (18.8%) infants and 26 (2%) newborns (28 days of age or less).

Table 2. Principal diagnostic groups, shown as percentages of total number in the audit of 1,282 randomly selected new attenders, of whom 241 were infants and 26 were newborns

Diagnostic group	Total (%)	Infants (%)	Newborns (%)
Trauma (including fractures)	37	12	0
Respiratory	22	42	32
Gastrointestinal	13	20	23
Dermatology	7	9	4
Neurology	4	2	4
Bone and joint	3	1	0
Genito-urinary	3	4	4
Ingestion/poisoning	2	0	0
Cardiovascular	0.7	1	4
Ophthalmic	2	2	8
Nutritional	1	2	4

Injuries and accidents

Accident or injury was the commonest reason for attendance. There were 451 accidents (35% of the sample), which resulted in 478 injuries.

The largest group of these (14.3%) occurred 'out and about' (in a public place), followed by home accidents (11.3%), with only 29 children (2.3%) injured either at school or sport. Road traffic accidents (RTAs) accounted for 22 patients (1.7%) but, not surprisingly, these tended to be more serious. Injuries were spread fairly evenly throughout the age groups, with the exception of infancy which comprised 18% of the sample but only 7% of the trauma. The sex ratio for those injured tended to be slightly higher (1.6) than the overall ratio quoted earlier, boys being much more likely to be injured in an RTA than girls ($p = 0.0001$) (M:F ratio, 3.8). Injuries at school and at sport showed a similar pattern ($p = 0.001$) (M:F ratio, 1.9). A seasonal trend was also apparent: 46.3% presented between May and September—almost double those presenting from November to March (23.8%). The opposite trend was seen with most other diagnostic groups.

Types of injury

Of the whole sample, 36.3% were soft tissue injuries and 4.6% fractures. The vast majority of the trauma cases (478 recorded diagnoses) were soft tissue injuries (97.2%), about one-eighth (12.3%) had a fracture and 9.6% were recorded as having both a soft tissue injury and a fracture. The commonest group of soft tissue injuries (84; 18%) was limb strains or sprains, divided equally between upper and lower limbs. There were 222 (46% of trauma) injuries to the head (including the face), but the skull was involved in only two of the 59 patients (about three daily) with a fracture (head injury: fractured skull ratio, 110). This further emphasises the infrequency of serious trauma. Almost half the fractures (46%) involved one of the forearm bones. Fractures of major limb bones were much less frequent.

Trauma admission rates

Admission rates for trauma varied enormously according to the type of injury and, as with medical or surgical illness, followed consultation with a registrar or consultant. Following RTAs, admission to hospital was significantly more likely than with other forms of trauma ($p = 0.0006$) (36% and 8.7%, respectively). The majority of injuries, however, were more minor. Thus, if RTAs are excluded, injured children were less likely to be admitted than those presenting with an illness ($p = 0.0009$) (8.7% compared to 16%). Only 6.5% of patients with soft tissue injuries were admitted, compared to 36% with a fracture. One-third of those with a fractured forearm bone required admission. Compared to those with other types of injury, children with a head injury were twice as likely to be admitted (4.3% and 9%, respectively).

Ingestions and poisonings

Ingestions and poisonings (23 cases) were much less frequent than fractures, and were generally uncomplicated. This may reflect a greater awareness of the dangers of drugs and chemicals within the household and the more widespread use of child resistant containers. Although 30% of these cases were admitted to hospital, this largely reflects a cautious approach, to which there may be an alternative (see below).

Respiratory disorders

The group of respiratory disorders was next most common (278 recorded diagnoses) and particularly frequent during the early months of life (Table 2). Not surprisingly, infections predominated: 52% of the 278 were thought to have an upper respiratory infection, two-thirds of which was pharyngo-tonsillitis, and 20% had a pulmonary infection, acute bronchiolitis being the most frequent (36%); 42 children presented with an asthmatic attack (15% of all respiratory disorders), making it the commonest reason for attendance after upper respiratory infection. Admission to hospital was required for 18% of those with a respiratory illness, including three-quarters of those with croup and 33% of patients with a lung infection, including bronchiolitis. One in five (21%) with an asthmatic episode was admitted, but in this small sample it was no more likely in those aged less than three years of age than in those who were older.

Gastrointestinal disorders

Gastrointestinal diagnoses were recorded 168 times (13% of sample) and were also common in infants (Table 2). There were 50 cases of bowel infection, but the commonest reason for attending was because of abdominal pain (47%), three-quarters of which was thought to be associated with significant constipation, on the basis of clinical features and abdominal radiology. In the majority, symptoms resolved on an aggressive management programme directed by a consultant, which would tend to support this contention. An acute abdominal emergency, including appendicitis, was thought to have been present in 13 patients. The overall admission rate was high (23%), with 62% of surgical emergencies admitted, 50% of those with unexplained acute abdominal pain, and 18% of those with a suspected bowel infection.

Dermatological disorders

Perhaps surprisingly, skin disorders were relatively common (93 recorded diagnoses; 7% of the sample). Nearly half (49%) were thought to have a skin (including wound) infection, and 18% and 16% papulosquamous and toxic or erythematous disorders, respectively.

A separate, prospective audit of skin disorders *per se* in 1990–91, however, showed that infections were not well recognised by junior doctors (59% concordance with the dermatologist's diagnosis). Hence the need for more education and the establishment of an open-access clinic at which patients can be seen by a consultant dermatologist within a few days of A & E attendance.[12]

Bone and joint disorders

There were 46 diagnoses of bone and joint disorders, many of which presented diagnostic problems especially to inexperienced doctors. Although infections were infrequent (two cases in sample), abnormalities related to walking or weight-bearing, such as irritable hip and other causes of limp, were relatively common (31; 70% of the group). Only 14% required hospital admission.

Neurological disorders

There were 51 neurological diagnoses, the commonest being seizures, headaches (generally severe, persistent and not easily relieved) or suspected intracranial infections, particularly meningitis (10). This was the group which had the highest percentage of patients (71%) brought into hospital.

Emergency ambulance calls

There were 61 calls in our sample to the emergency ambulance service. There were 35 (57%) patients under the age of three, 59% were boys (M:F ratio, 1.44) and 29 (48%) had sustained an injury, four of whom had a fracture. Only 13 (59%) of the RTAs came to hospital by emergency ambulance, of which 7 (4%) required admission, compared to 57% of the non-trauma patients. There were 17 (28%) with respiratory illness (mostly asthma) and 15 (25%) with neurological disorders (mostly seizures).

Patients brought by emergency ambulance were significantly more likely to be admitted to hospital (49%) than all others attending the department (13%) ($p = 0.00001$) or than GP referrals (30%) ($p = 0.005$). Those with a fracture were significantly more likely to be admitted to hospital than those with a soft tissue injury ($p = 0.016$), and patients with a neurological problem than those with respiratory or gastrointestinal illness ($p = 0.044$). On the basis of these data, use of the ambulance service seems to have been appropriate.[13]

Disposal (outcome)

Slightly over half (53%) of the 1,282 new attenders were sent home, just less than one-third (31%) asked to attend for review at A & E or an outpatient clinic, and 15% were brought into hospital. Infants were more likely to be admitted than older children ($p = 0.00004$) but, conversely, were significantly less likely to warrant review (Fig. 2). There was no difference in the proportions who were discharged home.

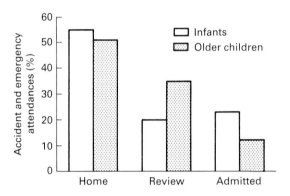

Fig. 2. *Outcome of accident and emergency attendances in patients less than 12 months old compared to those over 12 months; significant differences are shown for the percentages admitted and reviewed.*

Therapy in the accident and emergency department

The decision to administer therapy within the department will depend, *inter alia*, upon the nature and severity of the condition, and the existence of an effective therapy which it is practicable to administer and can reasonably be expected to act sufficiently rapidly to influence disposal. Acute asthma is the prime example where prompt administration of drug therapy by nebuliser may prevent admission to hospital. It may be, however, that a single treatment is insufficient, and daily therapy for several days is necessary to achieve this ideal.

Audit of treatment

The study showed that in the majority of cases (57%) immediate treatment was not required either in the department or from the GP.

This number was even higher in infants and newborns (Table 3). The type and range of therapies prescribed closely reflected the diagnoses of course. Thus, treatment for injuries (sutures, dressings, etc.) was required in 20% of attendances, an antipyretic in 7%, and inhalational therapy in 5%. Infants received proportionately less treatment for injuries and more for wheezing and infections, and newborns more dietary advice and ophthalmic preparations.

Table 3. Treatment prescribed for new patients in the accident and emergency department

	Total (%)	Infants (%)	Newborns (%)
None	57	62	73
Trauma (sutures, POP, strap, dressing)	20	5	0
Antipyretic	7	6	4
Nebuliser	5	9	0
Enema	3	2	0
Antibiotic	0.5	2	4
Dietary advice	0.5	2	8
Ophthalmic	1	1	4

POP = plaster of Paris

The quiet waiting area

Not all therapy, however, acts promptly, and some time may be required before it becomes clear what the appropriate disposal should be. Ideally, therefore, in each A & E department there should be a 'quiet waiting area' (in largely adult-orientated departments a room should be set aside specifically for children) where a period of nursing observation can be carried out. In addition to the benefit of observing a response to asthma therapy, such an area is appropriate for the first 5–6 hours' observation following certain head injuries, for some patients with epilepsy who have had a major seizure, in the management of the child with mild gastroenteritis has been started on oral rehydration therapy, and following emesis in less serious drug ingestions.

This is also an appropriate place to put the extremely irritable, febrile infant and his mother while the mollifying effects of antipyresis are being awaited—a situation the experienced physician would wisely prefer to reassess. An example is the baby who may have an exaggerated pyrexial reaction to a relatively trivial viral illness, the early stages of an encephalopathic disorder or a bacterial infection such as meningitis. This is also a preferable place in which to carry out test feeds, collect urine samples, etc. One staffed cot may perhaps be required per 8,000–10,000 annual new attenders. Units may differ as to how this area would operate—whether as a day unit, or short stay ward (e.g. 9 am to 5 pm), which we favour,[14] or as a 24-hour observation ward.

Who refers the patient?

Self-referral

It has already been observed that self-referrals constitute a large proportion of patients attending A & E departments. Striking differences in age, diagnosis and disposal will be highlighted between the self-referred and those referred by their GPs. Figure 3 illustrates the highly significant difference in age distribution, with the younger patients tending to be referred by their GP and those older than three years of age self-referred. Compared to patients presenting with injuries, those with medical or surgical diagnoses were significantly more likely to be referred by the GP (Fig. 4). Children with a neurological disorder were almost entirely GP-referred (see above); on the other hand, those with a dermatological problem were much more likely to self-refer. GP referrals were significantly more likely to be admitted to hospital than were the self-referred (Fig. 5).

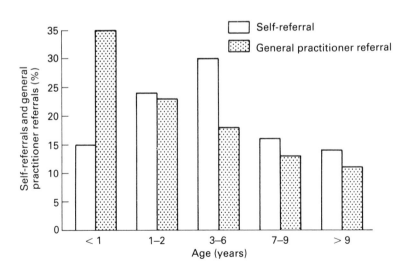

Fig. 3. *Age distribution of self-referrals and general practitioner referrals attending the accident and emergency department, showing a highly significant difference ($\chi^2 = 47.6$; $p = 0.00001$).*

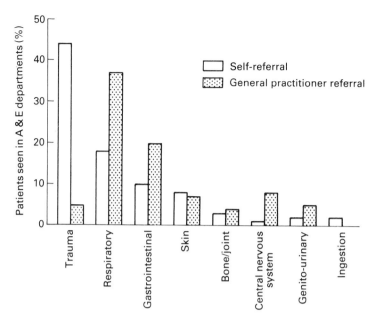

Fig. 4. *Diagnostic groups of patients seen in accident and emergency according to referral type* ($\chi^2 = 118.2$; $p = 0.0000001$).

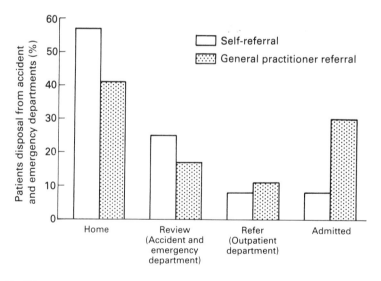

Fig. 5. *Disposal from the accident and emergency department shown in relation to referral source (parent or family doctor)* ($\chi^2 = 74.0$; $p = 0.000001$).

It would seem therefore that GP referrals tend to be infants and younger children with mainly medical disorders who are more likely to require hospital admission than self-referred patients who, broadly speaking, have minor injuries which rarely need admission.

General practitioner referral

To look at the problem from the GP's standpoint, in another study the total paediatric workload was prospectively audited in a predominantly social class III–V, three-doctor suburban family practice (total list approximately 6,000 patients). The study took place over a six-week period which happened to be midsummer. This practice has a very high proportion of children less than 13 years of age (2,500; 42%) 730 of whom required medical attention during the study period. Most of the patients (628; 86%) presented initially to general practice, 112 (18%) for inoculations, and the rest (102) to the A & E department. Of the 516 children seen by a GP with an illness or injury, the majority were dealt with at the health centre, only 23 needing referral to A & E for a second opinion (Table 4). Almost 96% of the non-trauma cases, including those for inoculations (68% if inoculations are excluded) presented to the GP, and only a tiny proportion (3%) were referred on (with another 5% referred to outpatients). Three-quarters (73%) of those who came directly to A & E had been injured, although the majority could have been dealt with in primary care, in that GPs treated 80% of children with similar injuries.[15] There is therefore enormous potential, particularly after minor injuries, for reducing the numbers of self-referrals to A & E departments.

Table 4. Number of children seen either in primary or secondary care during the six-week audit of 730 patients who required medical attention

	Non-trauma	Trauma
Presented to general practitioner	606	22
Self-referred to accident and emergency	28	74
Referred by general practitioner to accident and emergency	19	4
Self-referred to accident and emergency for second opinion	2	0

Inappropriate attendance

The complex area of inappropriate attendance is controversial, and demands sensitivity in our approach. An _appropriate_ visit might be one which follows a significant accident, injury or poisoning or is associated with a medical emergency. However, parents' perceptions of illness vary, and they may be uncertain where best to obtain medical help.[7] It is less certain how an _inappropriate_ attendance should be defined. A prospective study by Moira Stewart in 1984–85 specifically addressed this question.[7] An inappropriate visit was considered to be one that was based upon parental preference, where symptoms had been present for more than 24 hours, or where the family doctor was either unavailable, or had sent the child to A & E, unexamined or without contacting the department.

The study found that 36% of self-referrals were considered to have been inappropriate, although it should be stated that the perception of many parents was that their child urgently needed medical attention. However, only 6.3% had attempted to contact their GP before attending. It should be noted that 28% of GP referrals were also considered to come into this category, although this was different to the self-referral rate ($p < 0.05$). The explanation given for the self-referral was anticipation of onward referral to hospital by 122 parents (21%), and greater accessibility out of hours to emergency medical services by the others. However, more than half (56%) of the children did not in fact require any hospital resource (emergency treatment, X-rays, etc.).

The consultant early review

Although it is our aim promptly to refer back to the family doctor as many patients as possible, especially those who have self-referred, the role of the consultant review has an important place. Patients reviewed by the consultant will have attended in the previous one or two weeks with new problems, with conditions which have deteriorated abruptly or with more persistent disorders, especially where management is not being successful. Most referrals relate to vomiting or feeding in infants, wheeze, recurrent abdominal pain, seizures or limping, and less frequently headaches, usually in older children. Patients with skin disorders will have been referred to an open-access clinic (see above).

This arrangement provides an early opinion to inexperienced junior staff and to family doctors, who may in any case have made the initial referral (although obviously the system is open to abuse). It often obviates the need for further referral from A & E to an outpatient clinic or possibly admission to hospital. If reviews take place within the A & E department, the consultant is also available to give an opinion *pari passu* on the more acute problems in new attendances. Mornings are preferable for a review clinic as they suit mothers of school-aged children.[16] Such a clinic held two or three times weekly has a number of advantages:

1. It takes much pressure off a busy outpatient department.

2. Patients appreciate its immediate benefit, so failure to attend is unusual.[17]
3. The educational value to A & E junior staff is considerable, provided the review takes place when the referring doctor is on duty.

This approach is not appropriate, however, for those patients requiring long(er)-term management or the expertise of system specialists.

Implications and challenges

Assuming that the audit sample is reasonably representative of A & E paediatrics nationally, huge numbers of children with common medical and surgical conditions and injuries are seen each year (Table 5), the majority by specialists other than paediatricians. Our contention is that ways should and could be found to improve this unsatisfactory state of affairs:

1. Paediatricians should become more informed about their A & E departments, carry out an audit of the paediatric workload and consider its implications. They may also need to reconsider current arrangements for children who attend. This is especially important for those working in district general hospitals (DGHs) where the department may be largely adult-orientated.

Table 5. National estimates of the number of children attending accident and emergency departments annually based upon the 5.2% random sample, and assuming that in the UK there are 1.5 million new attendances

Upper respiratory infection (including otitis media, croup, etc.)	166,764
Asthma	48,451
Gastroenteritis/infective diarrhoea	57,680
Urinary infection	25,379
Seizure	25,379
Skin disorders	110,746
Cardiovascular disorders	10,377
Bone and joint problems	50,758
Head injury	256,099
Fractures	68,062
Ingestion/poisoning	26,496
Genital injury	3,460
Sudden infant death	probably 300*

* Based upon 5–6 brought to the department each year.

Ideally, there should be a separate children's waiting area, laid out, decorated and staffed by nurses with the appropriate training and experience. A play specialist should be part of the staff complement. Arrangements for coping with infants and the more ill children, cases of suspected child abuse and the families of sudden unexpected infant deaths or other child deaths, may need to be re-evaluated.

There should be a separate treatment room for children, and ideally a quiet waiting area or similar facility. Liaison health visitors must be attached by right to each A & E department, and outstanding shortages of junior medical staff urgently corrected.[1] Children should not be seen at departments which are remote geographically from the acute paediatric admission unit.

2. Colleagues scrutinising job plans might consider making some sessional commitment to their A & E department. How a paediatrician's time should be spent would depend upon local circumstances. Where staffing and facilities are improved overall, clinical management, especially of the acutely ill infant and young child, would follow. As diagnosis was sharpened and disposal more appropriate, hospital admissions might decrease. Bearing in mind that medical conditions and minor trauma constitute a very large proportion of the work, ways might be explored within an integrated child health service to involve clinical medical officers or SCMOs. These posts are currently under review, and a number of changes are envisaged which might facilitate cross-working between these complementary parts of community child health.[18]

The employment of GPs on a sessional basis ought surely to be phased out, since the lines of authority and control are often not secure and funding is expensive. These sessions would be more profitably redeployed, for example, as part of a vocational training scheme.

3. A paediatrician drafting the job description for a new consultant post in a DGH should give careful consideration to the creation of several fixed sessions in paediatric A & E medicine. Paediatricians working in centres with larger departments, seeing 18,000–20,000 new (child) patients annually, should press for some significant consultant input to the department—possibly a minimum of four to five sessions.

Nationally, the situation has improved since 1985 when there were only three full-time paediatric A & E consultants,[4] but it is still far from ideal. There are probably a number of other centres where such development would be appropriate. In some places, an alternative might be the creation of paediatric A & E staff grade posts, provided that there is a supportive working environment and the channels of communication and authority have been carefully established.

Bringing more paediatricians into A & E medicine would release colleagues, both registrars and consultants, from the disruptive effects of (repeated) calls to A & E, and the emergency care of children would improve. Medical education—undergraduate, postgraduate and continuing—to which Platt referred over 30 years ago would be enhanced (see recommendations 35, 36).[4] Indeed, we have found that there is a largely unmet demand for courses in A & E paediatrics, both for doctors in training and for the fully trained, especially GPs.

Although, as this chapter demonstrates, paediatric A & E audit can be greatly facilitated by computerisation of clinical records (although an A & E audit form has yet to be designed), its extension could lead to greater efficiency through application of the lessons learned. In addition, there should develop an appreciation of the potential for research—clinical, epidemiological and operational.

Finally, the importance of considerable job satisfaction, which paediatric A & E medicine affords, should not be overlooked or underestimated.

Space does not permit consideration of the self-referral question which urgently needs further study in liaison with specialists in general practice, epidemiology and community medicine in order to explore ways of reducing this costly duplication of primary medical services.

In the UK, all other branches of paediatrics and child health have already been well developed and standards of care advanced. The exception still remains paediatric A & E medicine, in spite of recommendations going back 25 years,[19] many of which were subsequently included in the Court Report.[20] This, then, is the challenge for paediatrics and paediatricians—the time is overdue for this Cinderella to meet her Prince Charming!

Acknowledgements

We would like to thank Dr C.C. Patterson, Department of Public Health and Medical Computing, The Queen's University of Belfast, for statistical advice, and Mr M. McCoy (Sherwood Systems Ltd) for computing expertise.

References

1. Jackson RH. Children in accident and emergency departments. *Br Med J* 1985; **291**: 991–2
2. Körner E (Chairman). *First Report to the Secretary of State of the Steering Group on Health Services Information.* London: Department of Health and Social Security, 1982
3. Wilkin W, Smith A. Explaining variation in general practitioner referrals to hospital. *Fam Pract* 1987; **4**: 160–9
4. Platt H (Chairman). *The welfare of children in hospital.* London: HMSO, 1959

5. National Association for the Welfare of Children in Hospitals. Where are the Children? An examination of regional statistics for children in hospital and their implications for agreed standards of care. In: *Caring for children in the health services*. London: NAWCH, 1987

6. Sherry M, Edmunds S, Touquet R. The reliability of patients in delivering their letter from the hospital accident and emergency department to their general practitioner. *Arch Emergency Med* 1985; **2**: 161–4

7. Stewart MC, Savage JM, Scott MJ, McClure BG. Primary medical care in a paediatric accident and emergency department. *Ulster Med J* 1989; **59**: 29–35

8. Wilson DH. The epidemiology of childhood accidents. In: *Proceedings of the Symposium on Accidents in Childhood (occasional paper no. 7)*. London: Child Accident Prevention Trust, 1985

9. Dean AG, Dean JA, Burton AH, Dicker RC. *Epi Info version 5: a word processing, database and statistics program for epidemiology on microcomputers*. Stone Mountain GA, USA: USD Incorporated, 1990

10. Jones CS, McGowan A. Self-referral to an accident and emergency department for a second opinion. *Br Med J* 1989; **298**: 859–62

11. Chambers J, Johnson K. Predicting demand for accident and emergency services. *Community Med* 1986; **8**: 93–103

12. Dolan OM, Glasgow JFT, Bingham A, Burrows D, Corbett R. *How well does the paediatric SHO recognise dermatological disorders?* 63rd Annual Meeting of the British Paediatric Association, Warwick, 1991

13. Davison AG, Hildrey ACC, Floyer AC. Use and misuse of an accident and emergency department in the east end of London. *J Roy Soc Med* 1983; **76**: 37–40

14. National Association for the Welfare of Children in Hospitals. Just for the day. Personal evidence presented to the Committee investigating children as day case admissions. In: *Caring for children in the health services*. London: NAWCH, 1988

15. McCann B, Bradley T, Glasgow JFT. *Paediatric referrals to primary and secondary care*. 64th Annual Meeting of the British Paediatric Association, Warwick, 1992

16. Partridge JW. Consultation time, workload, and problems for audit in outpatient clinics. *Arch Dis Child* 1992; **67**: 206–10

17. Andrews R, Morgan JD, Addy DP, McNeish AS. Understanding non-attendance in out-patient paediatric clinics. *Arch Dis Child* 1990; **65**: 192–5

18. British Paediatric Association. *Paediatric medical staffing for the 90s*. London: British Paediatric Association, 1991

19. British Paediatric Association, Standing Committee on Accidents in Childhood. Memorandum on the management of accidents in childhood. *Br Med J* 1967; **iii**: 103–5

20. Court SDM (Chairman). *Fit for the future: Report of the Committee on Child Health Services, vols 1 and 2. Command paper 6684*. London: HMSO, 1976

9 | Dealing with the sudden infant death syndrome

David Davies

Department of Child Health, University of Wales College of Medicine, Cardiff

Introduction

About 1,500 infants (about 2 per 1,000 births) in Britain are estimated each year to die suddenly, unexpectedly and, in spite of thorough autopsy, for no obvious reason.[1] Despite encouraging findings in recent years that the incidence has begun a downward turn, sudden infant death syndrome (SIDS) continues to be the commonest single cause of death in the first year of life after the first month. SIDS victims have a characteristic age distribution, with an almost total immunity in the first few weeks after birth and a peak incidence between two and five months. Ninety per cent of deaths occur under six months, most of them during sleep, boys succumb more often than girls, the incidence is higher in winter months, and poor housing, social under-privilege, smoking, inadequate antenatal care, low birth weight and young parents are often, but not invariably, associated risk factors.[2-4]

The grief to parents when their baby, previously well (or at most with minor symptoms of illness), is found dead is one of the most poignant and devastating of all human tragedies, leaving a memory never forgotten and indelibly imprinted on the minds of the parents for their lifetime. In western cultures, death is acceptable after either a period of illness or a particular lifespan. SIDS is particularly shocking in this context, with no prior illness, no lifespan and no explanation—it collapses the normal birth/death opposition very starkly.

The manifold problems that emerge require management in several phases. As soon as death has been diagnosed the parents, stunned and disbelieving, have to be helped through a maze of procedures and interviews, many of which expose the family as never before to intensive interrogation. The next phase is support and counsel to help the parents understand what has happened and, through grief, re-morse, guilt and anger, to come to terms with the dreadful reality of their loss, a process that can last many years—sometimes a lifetime. In this process other family members, parents and professional support groups (to name one in particular, the Foundation for the Study of

Sudden Infant Death), family doctor and health visitor, paediatrician and family counsellor, all have a role to play at various times. The third aspect of management involves guidance and support for the mother and father if they find themselves expecting another child, and the care and support of the baby in the early months following delivery.

It is this last aspect that I have chosen to discuss, with the aim of providing a practical framework of knowledge to help the professional worker deal with this very difficult problem in as coherent and sympathetic a manner as possible, with particular reference to recent research on physiological and anthropological risk factors which are being increasingly linked with the aetiology of SIDS.

A working model for sudden infant death syndrome

For the care of the mother and her next baby to be supportive, informative and, hopefully, reassuring, a working model is needed for the cause of sudden unexplained death. (Many mothers comment on how worried they are, given the current publicity, regardless of whether or not they have had or known a SIDS baby—so worried are some of them that this has sometimes been linked to post-natal depression.) This is extremely difficult for SIDS since neither its mechanism (pathophysiology) nor its aetiology is known. Inevitably, much has to be presumptive, speculative and guesswork, but at least there is agreement that there is no single cause of death—a fact which is especially important to make known to the parents very early on.

Respiratory controlling mechanisms

My own perception of the problem, an attempt to unravel complicated interacting strands that have been proposed to explain SIDS, is that death in SIDS victims is somehow related to failure of respiratory controlling mechanisms that ultimately leads to an insufficient respiratory drive. I believe that cardio-respiratory reflexes are especially involved and also chemoreceptor systems which, at a vulnerable developmental stage, normally serve to restore homoeostasis following the impact of destabilising forces on the control of breathing. This views SIDS more as a 'physiological syndrome' than a 'disease' in the accepted sense, an expression of maturational delay of neurological mechanisms.

An analogy understood by parents is that the delicate control and stability of breathing is like a tightrope walker with destabilising influences constantly acting to upset a delicate equilibrium, but with physiological adjustments equally active in counterbalancing them in normal circumstances. Any disturbance to this equilibrium can upset the control of breathing, leading in some instances to death. I believe further that in some babies unique combinations of destabilising forces and inadequacies of compensatory responses operate to provide a combination of stresses and circumstances that may be lethal, but that *in any individual baby these balances and imbalances are not known.*

I view epidemiological risk factors as being linked somehow with destabilising influences, such that if these can be avoided or modulated the risk of death should be lessened. The combination of destabilising forces are as pieces of a jigsaw puzzle: it is only when the puzzle is completed by individual pieces coming together that death will take place or, as Bergman has so eloquently put it:

> SIDS is like a nuclear explosion where a critical mass must be attained before the event is to occur.[5]

My approach (which I believe is appropriate for all infants) has as its focus preventing these fragments coming together by removing risk factors.

The aetiological model and risk factors

I will focus attention on several aspects which emerge from this aetiological model

- preventing illness (especially infections);
- smoking;
- the avoidance of an unduly warm environment for the baby;
- the use of apnoea alarms to alert parents to prolonged cessation of breathing;
- culturally associated infant care practices;
- sleeping posture;
- where the baby should sleep in the early months after birth.

Preventing illness

Minor symptoms of illness, such as snuffles, cough, fever or irritability, for example, and an increased number of visits to the general practitioner and health visitor are more frequent in SIDS victims than in live matched control infants.[6] However, the relevance of these associations to SIDS is not known. Infections of the respiratory passages of infants are very common as the baby comes to terms with living in an environment highly contaminated by micro-organisms. In my working model, these symptoms are considered either as destabilising influences to the delicate control of breathing or markers of these influences. It is, therefore, important to emphasise and promote the best possible health in the new baby.

Breast-feeding should be encouraged. In a recently published study from the USA of 757 SIDS victims and 1,600 control infants, about 10% of the former were mostly or only breast-fed compared with about 25% of control infants.[4] Other than in this particular study, though, breast-feeding itself has not been convincingly shown to protect against SIDS. (Indeed, in Hong Kong, where there is virtually no breast-feeding, there is an exceedingly low incidence of SIDS.[7]) Is it perhaps because breast-feeding is so closely linked with other associated epidemiological factors that are protective—for example, older age, higher social class, low smoking rates—that it has not been found more often on its own to protect, that its beneficial influences are being masked by other factors? Nevertheless, it would be wrong not to encourage breast-feeding because it allows the best chances of normal growth, optimum psychomotor development and the best possible health. At the same time, for those mothers unable or not wishing to breast-feed, careful attention must be given to substitute feeding practices. If babies become unwell for whatever reason, they should not be left alone for long periods, either by day or by night (a matter to which I refer later), and professional advice must be sought.

Smoking

Smoking has been irrefutably identified as an important risk factor, and this practice must be discouraged in parents and all household members both during and after pregnancy.[2-4] The mechanisms of the link are not known. Before birth, maternal smoking slows fetal growth, and after birth a smoky environment increases the risks of respiratory infection in the baby. Perhaps these are links in the chain. Other hidden social factors, some involving infant care, might also somehow be operating. Thus, in the same way that breast-feeding tends to be associated with higher social class and better socio-economic conditions, smoking is associated with lower social class and poorer conditions, and it is increasing among young women.

Overheating

It has been known for many years that some SIDS victims when found are very warm, implying that a heat stress may somehow play a part.[8] The mechanism(s) responsible are unknown, although it is conceivable that, in certain circumstances, high body temperatures may upset the delicate control of breathing. Interest in thermal balance has led research workers in Leicester to study patterns of temperature rhythms in babies in their homes.[9-11] They have been able to show that in the wide range of environmental conditions found in homes, with regard to room temperature, bedding, blankets, etc., the baby's temperature is remarkably little affected in the first six months of life. This is not to say, however, that some thermal stress does not sometimes take place: faster pulse rates and sweating have been shown to occur in some babies when the ambient temperature is high.[9,12] Another angle to the temperature story comes from population-based case-control studies in Avon by Fleming and colleagues, who have shown that babies who succumb to SIDS are more likely to have been more heavily wrapped than control infants, and to have been in a house with more heating at night.[13] A recent study has shown that younger mothers and mothers in lower social groups put more bedclothes over their babies and tend to prefer warmer room temperatures.[12] Based upon existing know-ledge, and recognising that much has yet to be learned about ideal conditions of insulation and temperature, it seems sensible advice not to allow babies to get too hot. The room in which the baby sleeps should be at a comfortable temperature—a temperature range of 16–20°C is reasonable. Swaddling in blankets and the use of thick duvets should be discouraged, several thin layers of blankets and sheets being preferable, with precautions taken to ensure that the head, the major radiator of body heat, is exposed. It is especially important to stress that babies who are unwell with a fever need fewer clothes to cover them. It is remarkable how consistent customs are worldwide to wrap up babies who are unwell.[12,14]

Apnoea alarms

The question of whether apnoea alarms should be used in the subse-quently born baby is always raised. Most apnoea alarms currently available for use in the home detect central and not obstructive apnoea. It is unproven whether they are able to detect hypoxaemic episodes, and there is no evidence that they save lives.[15] Babies have been known to die on monitors. These facts, however, are insufficient to assuage parents' demands for breathing monitors. They are more a lifeline, a source of comfort, a psychological prop, for parents rather than a help for babies, and form part of a wider strategy of support beginning at the birth of the next baby, when a thorough neonatal examination is done, links established with the parents, and definite arrangements made for the careful follow-up of both baby and mother. Detailed instructions on the use and limitations of apnoea alarms must be given, and on how babies should be resuscitated if they suffer prolonged apnoea. Every effort should be made to discourage their use for more than 9–12 months. It is all too easy for parents to become over-dependent on apnoea alarms.

Culturally associated infant care practices

One of the most intriguing associations of SIDS is its very varied geographical and ethnic incidence. For example, in Chicago from 1975–80 there was a much higher incidence in blacks (5.1 per 1,000 live births) than in whites (1.2) and hispanics (1.3).[16] Until recently the South Island of New Zealand had one of the highest incidences of SIDS in the developed world (7.6 per 1,000),[17] yet in Finland, a rate of only 0.41 per 1,000 was described in 1969–80.[18] A very low incidence was reported in Hong Kong in 1987 (0.29 per 1,000),[7] corroborating many unpublished clinical impressions of the rarity of SIDS among the Chinese and other ethnic groups in South-East Asia. In Japan, current published rates for SIDS are very low, of the order of 0.15 per 1,000.[19] In the USA, the lowest incidence has been reported among oriental Americans (0.51 per 1,000).[2] Of special interest is a study by Grether showing that the longer oriental families live in the USA, the greater becomes the risk of SIDS.[20] In England and Wales, two reports of infant deaths related to ethnic factors have shown that SIDS occurs significantly less often among infants whose mothers come from the Indian subcontinent than among those whose mothers were born in Britain.[21,22]

Some of these ethnic variations are paradoxical. Mothers born in Pakistan and Bangladesh who now live in Britain are reported poorer, have more children with shorter intervals between pregnancies, and live in less satisfactory housing than indigenous mothers—all factors that could conceivably be expected to increase the likelihood of SIDS.[21] In the Chicago study, Hispanics shared many adverse social and environmental factors with black families yet the incidence of SIDS was four times less.[16] The gross overcrowding, lack of breast-feeding and high incidence of respiratory tract infections in Hong Kong could be considered major risk factors.[23]

Is it possible, therefore, that protection may sometimes be conferred in the midst of potential high risk situations? Could culturally associated infant care practices provide an important clue? In 1985, commenting on the very low rates of SIDS in Hong Kong, I wondered whether the possible influences of life-style and caretaking practices on cot death, such as posture, are being underestimated in preference for more exotic and esoteric explanations.[23]

Sleeping posture

Following the observation in the 1980s that SIDS was very uncommon in Hong Kong where, as in other parts of South-East Asia, babies are placed supine (chiefly for fear of suffocation), there has been a lot of interest in recent years in the importance of the sleeping position to SIDS.[7,23,24] In reviews of available literature, Engelberts[25] and Fleming[26] have been unable to find any evidence for the supine posture being a risk factor for SIDS. The possibility of recall bias in the interview of bereaved parents providing spurious information has been raised, but prospective cohort studies in Avon,[13] Hong Kong[7] and Tasmania[27] now provide substantial information on links between sleeping posture and SIDS, showing that SIDS victims are more likely than control infants to have been sleeping prone.

The mechanism that might link the prone position with SIDS is not known. Might it relate to oro-pharyngeal obstruction or obstructive apnoea secondary to partial nasal obstruction? Could it be linked with thermal stress? A baby lying prone could find it harder to lose heat, since in this position it is easier for the baby to be lost amongst the blankets and less of the head be exposed. Wailoo and Peterson in Leicester have shown that in the prone position babies do have slightly more difficulty losing heat but, at the same time, they speculate that, even interacting with warm conditioning, lethal hyperpyrexia would be well-nigh impossible to achieve in otherwise normal babies.[11] If a baby lying supine becomes very hot, it can make attempts to rid itself of excessive clothing: this cannot be done in the prone posture. Fleming and colleagues have attributed a 40% reduction in cot deaths in 1990–91 in Avon to a change in parents' choice of sleeping position from prone to side/back.[28] Findings in Tasmania[27] and the Netherlands[29] are similar.

In our current state of knowledge, therefore, it seems sensible to advise mothers not to lie their babies prone, the back or side being preferred. The exceptions to this general statement are babies with the Pierre Robin syndrome and perhaps some with gastro-oesophageal reflux where the prone position offers greater advantages.

It would be wrong, however, to view this recommendation as truly original. A leading article on cot death in the *British Medical Journal* in 1971 concluded with these words:

> If death comes from a failure to cope with respiration difficulties it seems sensible to put a baby to sleep on his side or back rather than face down when the weight of the trunk and not merely that of the ribs and abdominal wall have to be lifted at each breath.[30]

This advice constitutes a '180° turn' from previous counsel, and it will be difficult to change practices overnight. (Mothers are often rather cynical about what they see as 'changing trends' and the amount of conflicting advice from midwives, doctors, etc., even in the same hospital.) The lateral position, with the lower arm placed well forward so that babies cannot roll on the stomach can be put to the mothers as a 'halfway house' if they are happier with this.

At the same time, it must be emphasised that there is no evidence that choking occurs more commonly in either of these positions, as is still often taught. It is important not to create undue anxiety—after all, millions of babies have slept prone with no deleterious effect. If, for example, a baby is generally more comfortable lying prone, as babies often are, this will have to be accepted, and care taken to avoid the potential threat of thermal stress, as previously mentioned. Bangladeshi mothers in Cardiff, for example, prefer the supine position because a rounded head is favoured (M. Gantley, personal communication).

Where the baby sleeps

Another culturally related factor is where the baby sleeps. I consider this issue to be very important, yet sorely neglected, and therefore make no apology for discussing it in some detail. Attitudes of infant care in western countries lead to very different sleeping environments for babies, often with long periods of solitude at a vulnerable time in the development of respiratory control. Between two and six months there appears to be an instability in the regulation of breathing (which possibly has part of its expression, even in healthy infants, in episodes of apnoea and periodic breathing).[31] Over this period, there also appears to take place a functional shift in the regulation of breathing as cortical brain mechanisms begin to dominate over earlier brain stem systems.[31] In this way, a primitive and relatively inflexible system is replaced by one in which some learning is required for its evolution.[31] In the animal world separating the young from the mother for long periods until weaning has been established is the exception: it is *Homo sapiens* that provides this exception. SIDS is also uncommon in societies where, for social or cultural reasons, babies are not left alone. Solitary sleep has come late in evolution, a point written about extensively by McKenna[31,32] and Lipsitt,[33] who see cot death more in an anthropological and developmental context. Their theme is that during this period of respiratory vulnerability tactile, auditory, thermal, chemical (changes in concentrations of respiratory gases in the infant's immediate environment), and vestibular sensory stimuli derived from the infant's micro-environment and entering the brain-stem reticular formation could have a function in helping to regulate respiration. The natural care-giving environment in which the human species, along with other mammalian orders, has evolved, with the young sleeping in close contact with the mother or other care-giver, provides cues optimally provided from a sensory rich environment—an environment of physiological adaptiveness perhaps to help stabilise breathing and diminish the chances of a respiratory crisis.

Our current urban, Western norm, however, provides a very different micro-environment for the young infant, with many babies typically placed for long periods in their own room and cut off from
contact with anyone. Sleeping in the same room in the early months
after birth is not generally encouraged, but sleeping alone inevitably
deprives young infants of much environmental sensory experiences.
During deep sleep, respiratory drive and rhythm seem to be especially
dependent on sensory input and chemical stimuli to override biological
deviations in breathing control.[31] If, for whatever reason, such a baby
has a lapse in breathing, there may be less opportunity for self-
correction. Indeed, Lipsitt has described SIDS babies as though they
had simply:

> forgotten to breathe, unable to arouse themselves to take the next breath
> and so continue the respiratory cycle.[33]

Infants at greater risk, for example, through respiratory infection,
premature birth, previous nervous system damage, might be expected
to be particularly vulnerable to these lapses. Prolonged periods of
separation may also blunt parental awareness of minor illness that,
undetected, may lead to a baby's demise. Further studies are needed,
not simply related to where the baby is found but related to the
cumulative sleeping places in the previous days or even weeks. Could it
be that on occasions loneliness or fear is one piece of the jigsaw in a
particular baby, one imbalance to the equilibrium of breathing that
could act as a trigger either in causing prolonged apnoea or in
interfering with the baby's physiological adjustment to this? It is often
the case that the baby is found dead in another room, although case-
control studies have not mentioned whether SIDS victims are more
likely to have been left alone—but have the right questions been
asked? Compared with other more exhaustively researched areas of the
SIDS mystery, the issue of where the baby slept in the weeks leading
up to death is poorly researched.

There is a serious dearth of information on the cultural diversity and
attitudes towards infant-rearing practices. Preliminary studies from
some of our ethnographic research on attitudes towards infant care in
Cardiff by Bangladeshi mothers and those by the Cardiff ethnic
majority are beginning to reveal a number of emergent themes.
Bangladeshi babies are rarely alone, rarely in a quiet environment,
including both day- and night-time sleep (a custom they share with
babies in Hong Kong). Among Welsh families there is more emphasis
on the baby 'getting used' to being alone, to adapting to parents'
commitments (M. Gantley, personal communication).

I agree with McKenna and Lipsitt that it is time to view cot death
more in a biological and anthropological context than simply as a

pathophysiological medical event, as is currently our wont. Might our widespread western habit of putting young babies to sleep alone for artificially conditioned lengthy periods be potentially harmful? Recent studies have suggested that where there is co-sleeping, frequent arousals are common and long consolidated sleep very uncommon.[32] In some instances, is cot death perhaps a cost to be paid for western parents' wish for privacy? It is surely unreasonable to expect a nine-month unique symbiotic pre-natal physical bond between mother and intra-uterine baby to be so abruptly and quickly severed. On a more practical level, being left alone for long periods could lead to a worsening of a minor clinical illness, such as a cold, snuffles or temperature which, if detected early, could be approached and dealt with. An enhanced physical presence might make the mother more sensitive to small changes in behaviour.

Enforced loneliness during the early post-natal months of development is undesirable in a biological and developmental context. I advise mothers to have their babies in the same room at night for the first 6–9 months of life, and that the cot where they sleep by day should also be close by. 'How close is close?', many mothers ask—perhaps within the baby's hearing distance?

Conclusion

This chapter has attempted to provide a basis for a suitable strategy to help mothers who are pregnant, both those with and without previous experience of SIDS. A note of caution should be raised. Many people, agencies and parent support groups, are now involved in this problem and provide general advice and counsel. A leader in this field is the Care of the Next Infant (CONI) funded by the Foundation for the Study of Sudden Infant Death, itself pivotal in so much of the research into the aetiology and management of SIDS. Those at the sharp end, the health visitors, are key workers. Unless we are careful, the scene is therefore set for confusing and conflicting advice. Our current state of knowledge allows little room for dogmatism. How can it be otherwise when we still have a very cloudy idea of the pathophysiological mechanisms leading to this terrible terminal event? It is necessary to steer a pragmatic and commonsense course, recognising above all that 498 of every 500 babies born will not be a victim of SIDS. The extremely low risk of recurrence of SIDS should always be reinforced to parents. It is essential to avoid an over-exaggerated concern and, with it, to create undue stress in the mother. If consistent, uniform, well-balanced advice can be given, the mother will hopefully be reassured as far as is possible, and can look ahead to the pregnancy and the new baby with optimism and enjoyment. If, on the other hand, the views that we express are too dogmatic, prejudiced and at variance with those of other self-help groups, then many problems, confusion and anxiety will be created. A major challenge to health education strategies is presented. Perhaps a first step is to be careful about using language which is not clear to non-health professionals; for example 'prone' and 'supine' can easily be replaced by 'front' and 'back'.

Call wrote in 1986:

> the shock, trauma and bewilderment of parents whose infants die of SIDS are matched only by the confusing number of hypotheses, postulated causes, feelings of consternation and puzzlement by paediatricians and others who have attempted to explain sudden infant death syndrome.[34]

We must all work to prevent our own emotions and puzzlement from taking away from the mother the joy and excitement of having her next baby.

Acknowledgements

I am grateful to Ms Madeleine Gantley for her helpful comments and criticisms in the preparation of this chapter, and to Mrs Lesley Poole for preparing the manuscript.

References

1. Milner AD. Recent theories on the cause of cot death. *Br Med J 1987;* **295**: 1366–8.
2. Kelly DH, Shannon DC. Sudden infant death syndrome and near sudden infant death syndrome. A review of the literature 1964–1982. *Pediatr Clin North Am 1982;* **29**: 1241–61
3. Golding J, Limerick S, Macfarlane A. *Sudden infant death: patterns, puzzles and problems.* Shepton Mallet, England: Open Books Publishing, 1985
4. Hoffman H, Damus K, Hillman L, Krongrad E. Risk factors for SIDS: results of the National Institute of Child Health and Human Development SIDS Co-operative Epidemiology Study. In: Schwartz P, Southall D, Valdes-Dapena M, eds. Sudden infant death syndrome: cardiac and respiratory mechanisms and interventions. *Ann NY Acad Sci* 1988; **533**: 13–31
5. Bergman A. *The discovery of sudden infant death syndrome: lessons in the practice of political medicine.* New York: Praeger, 1986: 17
6. Gilbert R, Fleming PJ, Azaz Y, Rudd PT. Signs of illness preceding sudden unexplained infant death. *Br Med J* 1990; **300**: 1237–9
7. Lee NNY, Chan YF, Davies DP, Lau E, Yip DCP. Sudden infant death syndrome in Hong Kong: confirmation of low incidence. *Br Med J* 1989; **298**: 721
8. Stanton AN. Overheating and cot death. *Lancet* 1984; **ii**: 1199–201
9. Wailoo MP, Peterson SA, Whittaker H, Goodenough P. The thermal environment in which 3–4 month old infants sleep. *Arch Dis Child* 1989; **64**: 600–4
10. Peterson SA, Anderson ES, Lodeman M *et al.* Sleeping position and temperature. *Arch Dis Child* 1991; **66**: 976–9
11. Wailoo M, Peterson SA. Bedding and sleep position in the sudden infant death syndrome. *Br Med J* 1990; **301**: 492–3
12. Bacon CJ, Bell SA, Clulow EE, Beattie AB. How mothers keep their babies warm. *Arch Dis Child* 1991; **66**: 627–32

13. Fleming PJ, Gilbert R, Azaz Y, Berry PJ, Rudd PT, Stewart A. Interaction between bedding and sleeping position in the sudden death syndrome: a population-based case-control study. *Br Med J* 1990; **301**: 85–9

14. Nelson EAS, Taylor BJ. Infant clothing, bedding and room heating in an area of high post-neonatal mortality. *Paediatr Perinatal Epidemiol* 1989; **3**: 146–56

15. Foundation for the Study of Infant Deaths and the British Paediatric Respiratory Group. Apnoea monitors and sudden infant death. *Arch Dis Child* 1985; **60**: 76–80

16. Black L, David RJ, Brouillette RT. Effects of birth weight and ethnicity on incidence of sudden infant death syndrome. *J Pediatr* 1986; **108**: 209–14

17. Borman B, Fraser J, de Boer G. A national study of sudden infant death syndrome in New Zealand. *NZ Med J* 1988; **10**: 413–5

18. Rintahaka PJ, Hirvonen J. The epidemiology of sudden infant death syndrome in Finland in 1969–1980. *Forensic Sci Int* 1986; **30**: 219–33

19. Tasaki H, Yamashita M, Miyazaki S. The incidence of SIDS in Saga prefecture (1981–85). *J Paediatr Ass Japan* 1988; **92**: 364–8

20. Grether JK. Sudden infant death syndrome among Asians. *J Pediatr* 1990; **116**: 525

21. Balarajan R, Soni RV, Botting B. Sudden infant death syndrome and post-natal mortality in immigrants in England and Wales. *Br Med J* 1989; **298**: 716–20

22. Kyle D, Sunderland R, Stonehouse M, Cummings C, Ross O. Ethnic differences in incidence of sudden infant death in Birmingham. *Arch Dis Child* 1990; **65**: 830–3

23. Davies DP. Cot death in Hong Kong: a rare event. *Lancet* 1984; **ii**: 1346–9

24. Lee N, Davies DP, Chan YF. Prone or supine lying for pre-term infants? *Lancet* 1985; **i**: 1332

25. Engelberts AC, de Jonger GA. Choice of sleeping positions for infants: possible associations with cot death. *Arch Dis Child* 1990; **65**: 462–7

26. Fleming PJ, Berry PJ, Gilbert R, Rudd PT. Bedding and sleeping position in the sudden infant death syndrome. *Br Med J* 1990; **301**: 871

27. Dwyer T, Ponsonby A, Newman N, Gibbons L. Prospective cohort study of prone sleeping position and sudden infant death syndrome. *Lancet* 1991; **337**: 1244–7

28. Wigfield RE, Fleming PJ, Berry PJ, Rudd PT, Golding J. Can the fall in Avon's sudden infant death rate be explained by the observed sleeping position changes? *Br Med J* 1992; **304**: 282–4

29. de Jonger GA, Engelberts AC. Cot deaths and sleeping position. *Lancet* 1989; **ii**: 1149–50

30. Editorial. Cot death. *Br Med J* 1971; **iv**: 250–1

31. McKenna JJ. An anthropological perspective on the sudden infant death syndrome (SIDS): the role of parental breathing cues and speech breathing adaptations. *Med Anthropol* 1986; **10**: 9–53

32. McKenna JJ, Moska S. Evolution and the sudden infant death syndrome. Part III. Infant arousal and parent-infant co-sleeping. *Hum Nature* 1990; **1**: 291–330.

33. Lipsitt JP. The importance of collaboration and development follow-up in the study of perinatal risk. In: Smeriglo, VL ed. *Newborns and parents: parent-infant contact and newborn sensory stimulation.* Hillsdale NJ: DJ Lawrence Erlbaum Associates, 1981: 135–5

34. Call J. Commentary on: McKenna JJ. An anthropological perspective on the sudden infant death syndrome (SIDS): the role of parental breathing cues and speech breathing adaptations. *Med Anthropol* (special issue) 1986; **10**: 565

10 | Recognising child abuse from accidents—fractures

Christopher Hobbs

Consultant Community Paediatrician, St James's University Hospital, Leeds

Introduction

Child abuse is neither an accident nor usually an emergency. Sooner or later it presents as a crisis, which may be an injury such as a fracture. Therefore, it is vital that after every injury sustained by a child we pause to think of the circumstances in which that injury has occurred. Child abuse is not a good term to describe the negative acts of omission in a child's care which we prefer to call neglect. Neglect is a factor present in most injuries to a varying degree. The all-encompassing term 'child maltreatment' is now gaining wider acceptance. In the context of parental care, child maltreatment has been defined as any interaction or lack of interaction between a child and his/her care parents which results in non-accidental harm to the child's physical and/or developmental state.[1]

The jigsaw model

It is important to emphasise that abusive interactions between parents and children are on-going processes linked to complex patterns of behaviour, which often have their roots in generational continuities and within the ways that members of families relate to one another. When we see a bruise, a fracture or a burn, for example, it is a symptom of a much wider problem. Understanding of this will require a combination of medical knowledge and skills with those of other professionals to piece together a wider picture. This model is termed the jigsaw approach, and through it a complete diagnosis and description will emerge. Critical aspects of the jigsaw puzzle in physical abuse diagnosis are shown in Fig. 1. The injury, for example a fracture or head injury, is frequently the presenting focus of concern but, if the history is reasonable and consistent, it is unlikely that there will be further questioning unless other pieces of the jigsaw are present, such as signs of obvious neglect or high levels of parental stress. Where the injury is not consistent with the history, we start to assemble the jigsaw

puzzle further and involve others, obtaining information from health
visitors, the family doctor, school, social services or police, etc.

In physical abuse, therefore, doctors are often the people to have the
first concerns, and one of their main decisions is whether to involve
others. However, no one can have all the pieces of the jigsaw and,
given more information, concern about an individual case may increase or diminish. Informal as well as formal systems for communication are essential for child protection. It should be possible to speak
to social services about a child without initiating a formal investigation.

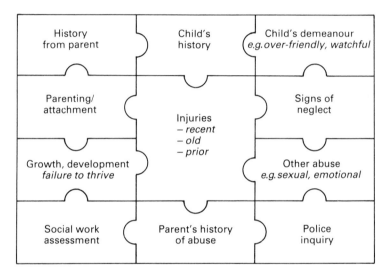

Fig. 1. *The jigsaw in physical abuse.*

Bony injury as an indicator of abuse

Abusive fractures usually result from the more extreme forms of
violence and represent serious injury. They may co-exist with other
signs of trauma, either external (bruises or scratches), or internal
(subdural haematoma, retinal haemorrhage or ruptured gut). Bony
injury in the presence of normal bones provides incontrovertible
evidence of substantial trauma, and historically is the basis for medicine's first acknowledgement of the existence of child abuse.

Caffey described infants with multiple skeletal injuries and with
subdural haematoma and retinal haemorrhage.[2] He noted that metaphyseal avulsion fragments from the ends of long bones appear to
result from:

> indirect traction, stretching and shearing, acceleration-deceleration stress
> on the periosteum rather than direct impact stress such as smashing blows
> on the bone itself (Fig. 2).

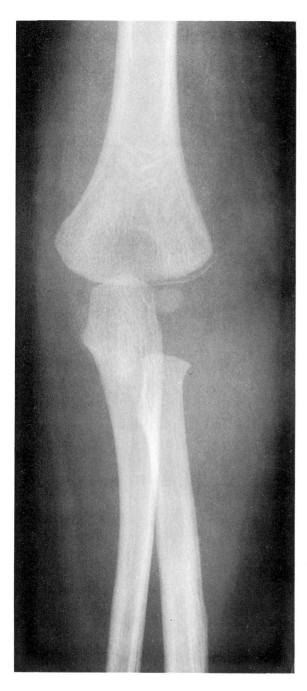

Fig. 2. *Meta-physeal (bucket handle) fracture of the distal end of the humerus in a 2-year-old child with other bruises and burns.*

He linked this to the whiplash shaking syndrome. Since then, the spectrum of injury to the infant and young child's skeleton has widened. Injury to almost every bone in the body has been described in abuse, but certain patterns have emerged, and our understanding of the relationship between cause and effect improved.

Prevalence of fracture: abuse—accident

In one study of physically abused children, 58% were under the age of 3 years and sustained 95% of the fractures.[3] Abuse of infants and toddlers is more likely to result in bony injury than abuse of teenagers. In non-abused children, 85% of fractures occur over the age of 5 years.[4] In the first year of life not only are fractures more common after assault but, looking at the total population of infants with fractures, they are more likely to be the result of abuse than at other times. A high index of suspicion is required. In a study of 34 infants up to 1 year with 55 fractures, 15 patients were injured from accidents and 19 from non-accidental causes.[5] Estimates vary that from one in eight[4] to one in two infants[5] with fractures have been abused.

It is also important to place fractures within the context of known accidental situations. Studies of known accidents in hospital wards or at home by Helfer,[6] Kravitz,[7] Nimityongskul,[8] and Levene and Bonfield[9] suggest that fractures are an uncommon outcome in the ordinary run of childhood accidents. Falls from up to 3–4 feet account for most accidents in infants and toddlers but the chance of fracture is low (1–2% or less). About half such fractures are uncomplicated, single linear fractures of the skull.

History

When fractures follow genuine accidents the child is usually presented promptly, there is a clear history of an accident, with development of immediate pain, loss of function and developing swelling. In abuse, the history of injury may be vague, inconsistent or absent, and medical attention is more likely to be sought for swelling or loss of function after a period of delay. Sometimes, discovery of the fracture may be unexpected, for example a rib fracture, in an X-ray taken for a medical cause or in a skeletal survey after bruising has been found.

Patterns of injury

The fracture which follows abuse may be single or multiple, recent or old, or a combination, and be found in one or more sites. Important patterns of injury include:

- single fracture, for example, humerus, with excessive unexplained bruising;
- multiple fractures, different stage of healing (classical battered baby) (Fig. 3);
- metaphyseal/epiphyseal injuries, which may be multiple as in whiplash shaken infant;
- rib fractures (single or multiple) (Fig. 4);

- periosteal new bone formation;
- skull fracture with intracranial injury.

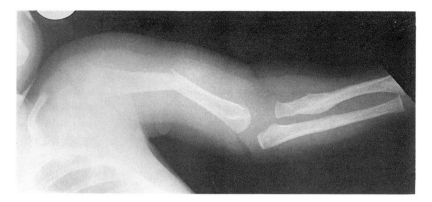

Fig. 3. *Recent humeral and old ulnar fractures in an abused 5-month-old infant.*

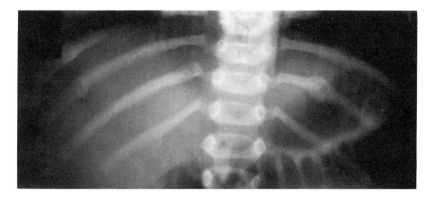

Fig. 4. *Healing rib fractures (left: 11th; right: 10th) in a 6-month-old infant.* In addition, there were skull, tibial and humeral fractures and many bruises.

Whilst injuries are never interpreted in isolation, they carry a different specificity for abuse. Injuries with higher specificity include wide complex skull fractures, metaphyseal and epiphyseal fractures, rib, scapula and sternal fractures, and multiple fractures. In contrast, narrow linear, usually parietal, skull fractures, fracture of the shafts of long bone, clavicular fractures or single injuries carry a lower specificity.

Types of fracture

Rib

In the absence of bone disease or a history of direct chest trauma rib fractures are due to physical abuse. Resuscitation has not been found to cause rib fractures.[10] They occur when the infant's thoracic cage is compressed and distorted during shaking, with the chest wall held firmly between the hands. The fractures are often multiple, bilateral and commonly posterior. Birth injury can be readily differentiated in most cases.

Metaphyseal

Disruption through the relatively more fragile growing part of the bone results from indirect trauma. The fracture appears in a corner or bucket-handle configuration, depending on the orientation of the X-rays, and usually a whole disc-like fragment results from complete separation. These injuries result from pulling or twisting forces and are often multiple. They have a strong association with non-accidental aetiology.[11]

Skull

Fractures of the skull are common in infants and young children and may follow falls. Patterns of injury in abuse tend to reflect the greater severity of injury when a child is thrown or swung against a hard object or punched when an adult is in a rage. Billmire and Myers found that 85% of serious intracranial injuries in children under 1 year of age were the result of abuse.[12]

The observable pattern of fracture in two groups of children (aged 0–2 years) in whom a fall was alleged, with accident or abuse separated by a range of considerations, showed significant differences (Fig. 5).[13] Abused children were more likely to exhibit multiple, complex or depressed fractures, wide (greater than 3 mm) and growing fractures, involvement of more than one cranial bone, and non-parietal fracture. Intracranial injury including subdural haematoma and a fatal outcome was more likely. Fracture of the occipital bone has a strong association with abuse, and a depressed fracture in this site is virtually pathognomonic of abuse (Fig. 6). Skull fracture correlates with an increased risk of intracranial haemorrhage. Therefore, in addition to the important forensic aspect, there are good arguments for X-raying the skull in head injury in childhood.[14] Severe head injury without impact or skull fracture can follow violent shaking episodes.

Dating a skull fracture is not possible in the way that fracture of bones formed in cartilage can be dated. The edges can become blurred, and the fracture line will eventually close in most cases, but the time sequence is variable.

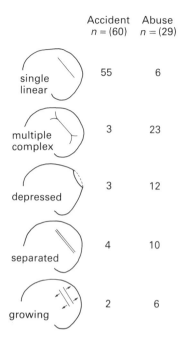

	Accident n = (60)	Abuse n = (29)
single linear	55	6
multiple complex	3	23
depressed	3	12
separated	4	10
growing	2	6

Fig. 5. *Skull fracture: anatomy (from ref. 13).* Observable pattern of fracture in two groups of children aged 0–2 years in whom a fall was alleged.

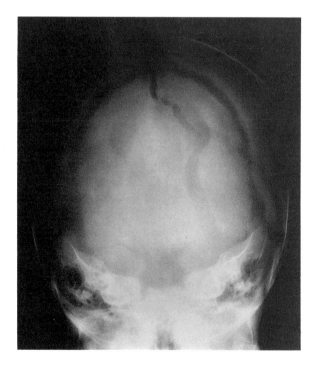

Fig. 6. *Extensive, wide and growing occipital fracture with associated subdural haematoma and cerebral injury in a 3-month-old abused infant.*

Long bone

Worlock *et al.* described 35 children with abusive fractures and 826 with accidental fractures.[4] They commented that long bone injuries strongly associated with abuse were subperiosteal new bone formation and spiral or oblique fractures resulting from gripping or twisting. In their study, spiral fracture of the humerus was significantly more common in abuse than in the control group. However, they concluded that the fracture alone in most cases would not enable differentiation.

The mechanisms of production of the four basic types of linear fracture are discussed by Alms.[15] This may be useful in checking the validity of a history. He concludes that the mode of production of the four basic types of fracture is deduced on the grounds of simple mechanical theory:

- *transverse* fractures are a result of angulation;
- *oblique transverse* fractures are the result of angulation with axial loading;
- *spiral* fractures are the result of axial twists with or without axial loading;
- *oblique* fractures are the result of angulation and axial twisting in the presence of axial loading.

Axial loading applies to bones, for example, the tibia, which are weight-bearing at the time of injury.

Figure 7 shows a single forearm fracture involving the radius and ulnar which might have occurred from the child falling, trapping her arm in a chair as she fell. In fact, bruising to the thigh and a pattern of failure to thrive increased concerns. Abuse by swinging the child by arm was later admitted. In both situations, though, angulation without axial loading could have produced the injury.

Femoral fractures have had a long association with child abuse. They account for about 20% of fractures seen in abused children, so a knowledge of these injuries is important. Age is an important variable influencing the likelihood of abuse versus no abuse in this type of fracture. Child abuse predominates as a cause in infancy. Among 117 children with 122 femoral fractures, Anderson found 18 under 13 months of age, of whom 15 (83%) were abused.[16] Up to the age of 2, 79% were abused, in two-thirds of whom the fracture was the only injury. In older children, the proportion of femoral fractures due to abuse falls. Thus, in a group of 74 children up to 6 years of age, abuse was identified in 34 (46%) but in 65% of infants under 1 year.[17]

Obviously it may be difficult to make a sufficiently certain diagnosis of abuse when a fractured femur is the only injury, but it is important to remember that trivial injury is unlikely to cause a fracture in an otherwise healthy child. In abuse, the fracture usually occurs during violent twisting or swinging of the leg or of the child by the leg. A spiral fracture of the shaft could occur accidentally, but only a major fall

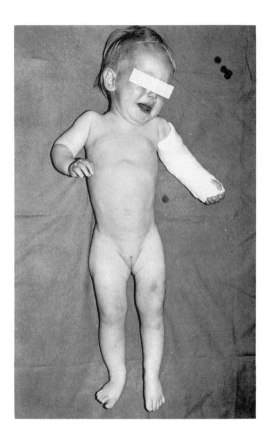

Fig. 7. *Mid-shaft fracture of radius and ulna in a 14-month-old girl with old bruising to thigh and failure to thrive.* Co-habiting boy-friend of girl's mother admitted to swinging child by arm.

would generate sufficient force to produce this injury. Thus, the injury shown in Fig. 8 in a 3-month-old child is unlikely to have occurred in the way the mother described. She said that she turned the child during feeding from one side to the other, catching his leg between hers in the process. This infant was also failing to thrive. Metaphyseal fracture occurs more often at the distal than the proximal end.

Spiral fractures of the tibia, once thought to be suggestive of abuse, are also thought to occur in the process of a toddler learning to walk. Metaphyseal fractures and periosteal new bone formation are more common in the tibia. Again, the history and other aspects will be important.

Spine

Spinal fracture is uncommon in children, but has now been described in the abuse literature in over 40 cases. Hyperflexia, hyperextension or

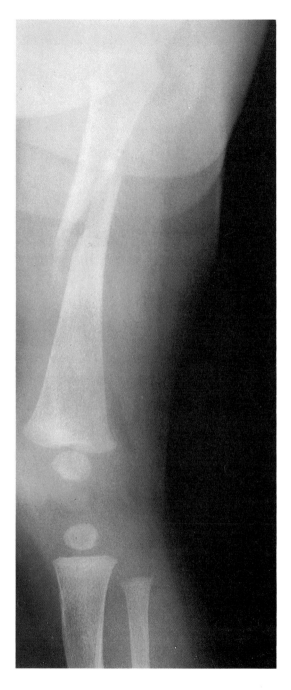

Fig. 8. *Spiral fracture of femur in a 3-month-old infant, whose mother said that as she turned the child during feeding she caught the leg.* Infant's weight below 3rd centile for age. Abuse thought probable.

the acute lateral flexion accounts for most of the injuries. Fracture of the vertebral bodies, usually lower thoracic or upper lumbar, are most often described. Unless there is a history of major trauma, such as road traffic accident, such findings are highly suspicious of abuse. Radiologically, anterior superior notching of the bodies due to herniation of the nucleus pulposus into the vertebral body, and narrowing of the disc space are characteristic. Acute kyphosis, vertebral dislocation, cord damage and paraplegia have all been described.

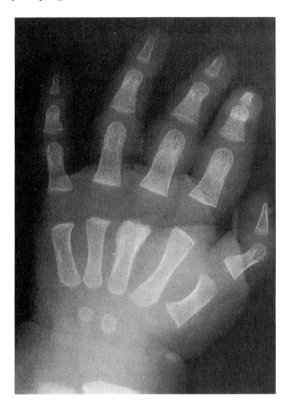

Fig. 9. *Unsuspected healing fracture of the metacarpal of the middle finger revealed on skeletal survey in an infant who presented with unexplained skull fracture.* This injury was also unexplained.

Skeletal survey

It has been our practice selectively to request a skeletal survey when physical abuse has been diagnosed or suspected. A skeletal survey should be considered in the following situations:

- when a child presents with a fracture which suggests abuse;
- in all physically abused children under 3 years of age;
- in older children with severe soft-tissue injury;
- when there is localised pain, limp or reluctance to use a limb;
- with a previous history of recent skeletal injury;
- when there are unexplained neurological symptoms or signs;
- in suspicious and unexplained death.

Carty suggests that the following radiographs are required when conducting a survey for occult trauma:[18]

- skull, anteroposterior and lateral views;
- chest, spine and pelvis anteroposterior views (on one film);
- anteroposterior view of long bones including the hands.

It must be emphasised that these are the minimum radiographs, and must be supplemented with local views of any suspicious area to establish a firm diagnosis.

Ageing or dating fractures

There is a wide range of time for the sequence of events which occur following bony injury, which is of obvious importance medico-legally. As an approximate guide, it should be noted that:

- a fracture without periosteal new bone formation is usually less than 7–10 days old, and seldom as much as 20 days;
- a fracture with definite but slight periosteal new bone formation could be as recent as 4–7 days;
- a 20-day old fracture will always have well defined periosteal reaction and typically soft callus;
- a fracture with well developed periosteal new bone or callus is more than 14 days old.[19]

Differential diagnosis

It is important to be aware of the infrequent alternative diagnoses other than a diagnosis of accidental or abusive injury. Birth trauma may be responsible for a fracture of the clavicle, usually mid-shaft. This fracture is sometimes found in an infant incidentally, in whom the birth trauma was not appreciated at the time. The history will help to differentiate breech injuries which are associated with metaphyseal fractures.

The risk of confusing osteogenesis imperfecta and the skeletal lesions of copper deficiency with child abuse have been overstated by those who would seek to deny child abuse in the legal setting. Classic cases of osteogenesis imperfecta, with a family history, clinical and radiological features, presenting in early infancy are very unlikely to be confused. Taitz discusses the chances of encountering the disease in a milder form under the age of 1 year as between 1 in 1 million and 1 in 3 million in a city the size of Sheffield.[20]

The diagnosis of copper deficiency requires establishing predisposing factors (prematurity, preceding malnutrition, deficient copper intake, malabsorption), and the presence of other clinical factors of copper deficiency (skin rash, hypotonia, hypopigmentation, psychomotor retardation), together with neutropenia, anaemia and low plasma copper concentration. Characteristic skeletal changes in copper deficiency include cupping and fraying of the metaphysis of long bones and sickle-shaped metaphyseal spurs. The entire skeleton is involved symmetrically, particularly at growing areas such as the wrists and knees. There are obvious similarities here with the other metabolic bone diseases, scurvy and rickets. The subject is well reviewed by Shaw.[21]

Conclusions

Differentiating accidental from abusive fractures requires a knowledge of the likely causation of the different injuries. Confirmation, to the level of the balance of probability required for child protection, follows the building up of a jigsaw puzzle which involves a co-ordinated multidisciplinary assessment tested at a case conference. The cause of all injuries cannot be accurately diagnosed, but involvement of paediatricians with experience of working in child protection is recommended with all children under 5 years of age who have fractures.

References

1. Helfer RE. Child abuse and neglect assessment, treatment and prevention. In: *Child Abuse Neglect* 1991; **15** (suppl 1): 5–15
2. Caffey J. On the theory and practice of shaking infants. *Am J Dis Child* 1972; **124**: 161–9
3. Herndon WA. Child abuse in a military population. *J Paediatr Orthop* 1983; **3**: 73–6
4. Worlock P, Stower M, Barbor P. Patterns of fractures in accidental and non-accidental injury in children: a comparative study. *Br Med J* 1986; **293**: 100–2
5. McClelland CQ, Heiple KG. Fractures in the first year of life. A diagnostic dilemma? *Am J Dis Child* 1982; **136**: 26–9
6. Helfer RE, Slovis TL, Black M. Injuries resulting when small children fall out of bed. *Paediatrics* 1977; **60**: 533–5
7. Kravitz H, Driessen G, Gomberg R, Korach A. Accidental falls from elevated surfaces in infants from birth to one year of age. *Paediatrics* 1969; **44** (suppl): 869–76
8. Nimityongskul P, Anderson L. The likelihood of injuries when children fall out of bed. *J Paediatr Orthop* 1987; **7**: 184–6
9. Levene S, Bonfield G. Accidents on hospital wards. *Arch Dis Child* 1991; **66**: 1047–9
10. Feldman KW, Brewer DK. Child abuse, cardiopulmonary ressuscitation and rib fracture. *Paediatrics* 1984; **73**: 339–42
11. Kleinman P. Skeletal trauma. General considerations. In: Kleinman PK, ed. *Diagnostic imaging of child abuse*. Baltimore MD: Williams and Wilkins, 1987: 5–28
12. Billmire M, Myers P. Serious head injury in infants. Accident or abuse? *Paediatrics* 1985; **75**: 340–2
13. Hobbs CJ. Skull fracture and the diagnosis of abuse. *Arch Dis Child* 1984; **59**: 246–52

14. Eyre J. Treating head injuries in childhood. (this publication)
15. Alms M. Fracture mechanics. *J Bone Joint Surg (Br)* 1961; **43**: 162–6
16. Anderson WA. The significance of femoral fractures in children. *Ann Emergency Med* 1982; **11**: 174–7
17. Gross RH, Stranger M. Causative factors responsible for femoral fractures in infants and young children. *J Paediatr Orthop* 1983; **3**: 341–3
18. Carty H. Skeletal manifestations of child abuse. *Bone* 1989; **6**: 3–7
19. O'Connor J, Cohen J. Dating fractures. In: Kleinman PK, ed. *Diagnostic imaging of child abuse*. Baltimore MD: Williams and Wilkins, 1987: 103–13
20. Taitz LS. Child abuse and osteogenesis imperfecta *Br Med J* 1987; **295**: 1082–3
21. Shaw JCL. Copper deficiency and non-accidental injury. *Arch Dis Child* 1988; **63**: 448–55

11 | Bruises and burns: accidental or non-accidental

Nigel Speight

Consultant Paediatrician, Dryburn Hospital, Durham

Introduction

The differential diagnosis between innocent accidents and inflicted injuries, or non-accidental injury (NAI), is one of the most difficult and important areas in general paediatric practice. Mistakes can have disastrous consequences for the child, the parents and even the paediatrician. For these reasons, it is desirable to approach each new case with an open mind, free of pressure of time and other duties. Unfortunately, in the real world the paediatrician is often asked to make a snap decision in the middle of a busy clinic. Such pressures should be resisted.

If a paediatrician diagnoses NAI in the case of an innocent accident, this constitutes a gross injustice to the family and, at worst, could lead to the removal of the child, with less unjust scenarios including the family living together under a cloud of professional suspicion and concern. No paediatrician in his or her right mind could view such happenings with anything other than horror. Accordingly, there is a natural initial bias to believe parents' accounts of accidents and, failing that, to give parents 'the benefit of the doubt'. For this reason, I believe that by far the commonest error in this field is the opposite one of failing to diagnose NAI when it exists.

The possible results of failure to diagnose NAI are, if anything, more serious. These include the following:

- the child may subsequently be killed;
- the child may be injured again and suffer brain damage;
- professionals may miss an opportunity of rescuing the child from a life of chronic emotional abuse and deprivation;
- the perpetrator/parent may be gaoled because of a further, possibly more severe, episode of abuse, and a potentially treatable family broken up;
- the paediatrician who made the mistake which led to the child's death may be forced into early retirement;
- if abuse is not diagnosed, the family cannot receive help, and further abuse is likely.

All but one of these are fortunately quite rare, but the third is, in my opinion, very common.

When all these alternatives are considered, the wise paediatrician will resolve to take the utmost pains to ensure a diagnostic accuracy as close to 100% as is humanly possible in this difficult area. Other, less honourable alternatives include avoidance reactions (for example, leaving it to junior staff or being generally unavailable) or sitting on the fence. Neither device does any service to the child or the family.

One comforting principle for paediatricians is that the *management* of the family does not automatically follow on from the diagnosis of NAI because non-accidental injury is not a full diagnosis, but merely a *symptom* of a disordered family.

The degree of danger is proportional to the severity of the under-lying disorder, *not* to the severity of the initial injury. The *management* of the case depends on the understanding of the family dysfunction, which is the responsibility of the social workers. Ideally, at the case conference the paediatrician's diagnosis and the social worker's family assessment should 'fit' each other—if they do not, both parties should think again.

Referral and assessment of suspected non-accidental injury

Front-line professionals (family doctors, teachers, relatives, casualty officers) will have all the horror already referred to of misdiagnosing an innocent accident as NAI. They should be reassured that their duty is simply to refer 'suspected NAI' to a paediatrician, who has to take the responsibility for definitive diagnosis. In such a two-tier system it must be accepted that some innocent accidents will be referred. If this were not the case, it would suggest that the threshold for referral is too high and some genuine NAI is being missed. 'Innocent families' so referred can hopefully accept the system as the price society must pay if children are to be protected and rescued.

Degree of proof required for final diagnosis

There are two standards of proof operating in the field of child abuse in court proceedings:

1. For criminal proceedings: *proof beyond all reasonable doubt.*
2. For civil proceedings: diagnosis *on the balance of probabilities.*

Paediatricians should not be hypnotised by the possibility of crimi-nal proceedings, which are relatively rare. In the vast majority of child abuse cases, it is diagnosis on the balance of probabilities which is required, on which it is much easier for the paediatrician to reach a judgement.

Advantages of admitting suspected cases to a paediatric ward

As already argued, at the end of the day it is vital that the paediatrician 'gets it right'. It will often be impossible to reach a conclusion at the first impression. The paediatrician would then be faced with making a snap judgement with potentially harmful consequences. Far preferable is a policy of admitting *suspected* NAI to a paediatric ward for further assessment. The advantages of this include:

- it gives the paediatrician *time* to consider before committing him or herself;
- the child's growth and behaviour can be assessed at leisure;
- the ward is a place of safety for the child;
- further accounts of how the injury occurred can be considered;
- blood tests, skeletal survey and photography can be performed;
- parents can have access to the child and/or be resident;
- nursing observation of the parent–child interaction and visiting pattern can be invaluable;
- the child may have the opportunity to disclose to professionals;
- no important decisions need to be made until the case conference.

In my experience, admission to the paediatric ward is invaluable in a significant proportion of cases in children of all ages, and has been the single most important measure responsible for 'getting it right'.

Unfortunately, admission to a paediatric ward for the above reasons appears to be going out of fashion despite its manifest advantages. The fashion is perhaps led by the teaching hospitals where beds are full of children with serious organic illnesses, and there is a feeling that child abuse is not 'proper' paediatrics. The resultant fashion for 'managing child abuse in the community' is, in my opinion, often a euphemism for covering it up.

Pointers to the diagnosis of non-accidental injury

It is worth remembering that in a strange way abusive parents *want to be found out* so that they can be helped out of their predicament, otherwise there would never be an opportunity to diagnose abuse in the first place.

The following pointers are useful guidelines, but none of them is foolproof.

1. Delay in seeking medical attention. This is easily understandable as the abusive parent hopes to avoid detection and indulges in wishful thinking, for example, that the leg is not really broken. The next day the child still cannot walk, and reluctantly the parents report to casualty.
2. The account of the 'accident' is not compatible with the injury observed. Examples include:

- 'I think he got it from lying on his dummy';
- 'The bruise on his forehead just came up while I was watching'; and
- 'He just brushed against my cigarette, honest.'

3. The account may be vague and lacking in detail. (Vivid, detailed accounts tend to have the 'ring of truth'.) The account may vary with each telling, and from person to person.
4. The parents' affect may be abnormal. They may lack normal anxiety for the child's injuries, be preoccupied with their own concerns and appear suspicious and/or aggressive.
5. The parents' behaviour may be abnormal, for example, in disappearing without saying anything or before seeing the consultant.
6. The parent–child interaction may be abnormal.
7. The child may be failing to thrive, apathetic, frightened or sad. 'Frozen watchfulness' is a late and very serious sign. Its absence, however, does not exclude the diagnosis of NAI.
8. The child may say something!

Case histories (*See illustrations on page 101*)

Case 1

A two-year-old boy was referred with a black eye, which the paediatrician decided was probably non-accidental in origin. The family situation was grossly abusive but, despite this, the child was returned home with supervision. There was no further episode of NAI in the next five years. Unfortunately, the emotional abuse and deprivation of which the black eye was symptomatic had continued unabated, and by the age of seven years he was diagnosed as severely emotionally damaged and virtually untreatable by a child psychiatrist.

Case 2

This two-year-old girl was brought to medical attention with a bruise over the shoulder blade which was diagnosed as probably non-accidental. She was kept in the paediatric ward pending the case conference. Parental visiting was very infrequent, and the parents showed little interest in the child when they did visit. The girl showed marked affection-seeking behaviour towards the medical and nursing staff and little interest in her parents. Although speech was retarded, there was no evidence of growth or other developmental retardation.

The court, the guardian, and subsequently a child psychiatrist all agreed with the presumptive diagnosis of severe emotional deprivation and the child was placed with foster parents with a view to adoption, where she thrived very satisfactorily. It is unlikely that intervention

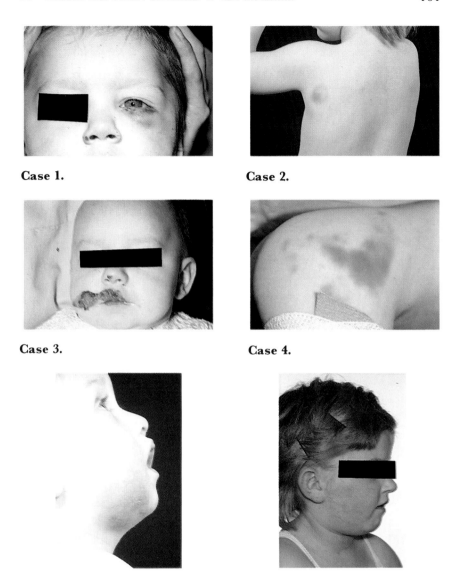

Case 1.

Case 2.

Case 3.

Case 4.

Case 5.

Case 6.

would ever have been initiated without the initial crisis resulting from the relatively trivial episode of NAI.

Case 3

A baby girl was brought to casualty with a dramatic lesion to her upper lip. This case showed many of the 'pointers' to the diagnosis of NAI listed above:

- there was a three-day delay in seeking medical treatment;

- the account given of an accident was incompatible with the injury observed (said to have been caused by accidentally brushing against a hot iron);
- different family members gave wildly different accounts of when the injury had occurred;
- the mother left the child in hospital and hardly visited.

The entire extended family colluded to protect the perpetrator, and the child was eventually removed for adoption.

Case 4

A four-year-old boy was admitted with a fractured femur said to have been caused by falling downstairs. Father gave out such hostile vibrations that no one felt like questioning him too closely, despite the multiple bruising to the hips and the child's wasted and frightened appearance. The boy was admitted, and placed in Gallows traction. The next day he said to a nurse, 'Daddy threw me downstairs'. On investigation, he was found to be under a care order for previous severe abuse, and had been 'rehabilitated' eight months earlier following the breakdown of a foster placement. The father was arrested while trying to remove the traction so that he could take the child out of hospital. He subsequently received a jail sentence, and the child was placed for adoption where he did very well.

Case 5

A child was coincidentally admitted to a paediatric ward generally unwell and feverish. A tense bruised area was noted over the right jaw and NAI suspected because the parents could give no account of an accidental cause. The child continued to run a swinging pyrexia, had a marked leucocytosis and eventually the blood culture grew *Haemophilus influenzae*. The diagnosis was changed to haemophilous cellulitis and the case conference cancelled.

Case 6

A six-year-old girl was admitted with apparent cellulitis to the cheek. The next day linear petechiae with tramlining were noted in the swelling, and it was concluded that she had been 'flat handed'. Neither parent could account for this and an NAI investigation started, with the girl kept in the ward pending the case conference. She resolutely refused to say who had hit her. Eventually it transpired that she had been hit by a ten-year-old boy who had sworn her and all the witnesses to secrecy! The case conference was cancelled and the parents bore no hard feelings.

Case 7

A seven-year-old boy from a problem family was referred with multiple bruising, which he said had been inflicted by his mother. Routine blood tests revealed idiopathic thrombocytopenic purpura with a dangerously low level of platelets. The parents were markedly ungrateful when he was cured of this!

Case 8

A $2\frac{1}{2}$-year old girl was referred from casualty with a black eye. She was admitted with no clear diagnosis, but subsequently the nurses felt she was frightened of her father and the diagnosis of NAI was considered. On taking more of a history, it transpired that the 'black eye' had been present for three months. On palpating the abdomen, multiple masses were felt. She turned out to have neuroblastoma. (Leukaemia is another condition which can be initially misdiagnosed as NAI, which is an extreme way of 'adding insult to injury'!)

In all these cases, except for Case 1, the admission of the child to the paediatric ward was crucial in elucidating the correct diagnosis.

Conclusions

The differential diagnosis of accidental from non-accidental injury is a crucial part of mainstream clinical paediatrics. Time, experience, open-mindedness and persistence are all required, and admission to a paediatric ward can be extremely useful.

12 | Is neglect neglected?

Leon Polnay

Reader in Child Health, Queen's Medical Centre, University Hospital, Nottingham
(This paper is reproduced by permission of Churchill Livingstone, from Community Paediatrics, second edition, 1992)

Introduction

Nearly all 'accidents' contain an element of neglect by exposure to risk, except those accidents which are true acts of God. Some would argue that these, too, can be avoided by appropriate action.

Neglect is a dilemma for me, in that it forms a great part of my work, and I can see problems with management, prediction and prevention. I also have problems dissecting out neglect:

- as a wilful act of omission;
- as a consequence of poor skills;
- as a variable in socially acceptable behaviour;
- in terms of poverty, disadvantage and resources; and
- in terms of reversibility or change in neglecting families.

Problems also arise because people (courts, social workers, etc.) think I can sort out all the above things.

This chapter addresses the issue of outcomes from different standards of parenting, and how these outcomes may be improved by intervention programmes. A child's health, development and emotional well-being depend upon a range of interactive factors. It is difficult, if not impossible, to weigh the relative importance of each of these factors against each other, yet it is a central task of the child health services to promote the health of children.

Influences upon child health, development and well-being (Fig. 1)

Definition of neglect

The definition of neglect for the purpose of child protection registers may be taken from one of the working papers of the Children Act, 1989:[1]

The child is suffering or is likely to suffer from abuse due to:
Neglect: the persistent or severe neglect of a child (for example, by exposure to any kind of danger, including cold or starvation) which *results* in *serious* impairment of the child's health or development, including non-organic failure to thrive.

Registration is therefore for the consequences of neglect and not for the act of neglecting itself.

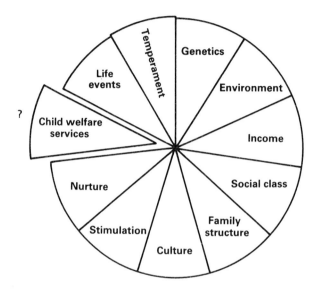

Fig. 1. *Influences upon child health, development and emotional well-being.*

Profile of neglecting parents

A profile of neglecting parents is shown in Table 1 (from reference 2). The features that follow this neglect include:

- poor diet and growth, leading to impaired learning ability, nutritional deficiency states and increased infections;
- a failure to protect from environmental hazards, leading to an excess of accidents;
- a failure to stimulate and teach, resulting in impaired educational achievement; and
- a failure to provide emotional warmth and affection, resulting in impaired social functioning.

Disadvantage, inequalities and neglect

There must obviously be diversity in the health of children and in their levels of attainment. The range, however, is very wide, and is determined more by social factors than biological factors. 'Inequalities' in

Table 1. Abusing and neglecting families (after Crittenden[2])

	Neglecting families	Neglecting & abusing families
Skills	Illiteracy common Depression common Unemployment common	Wider range of skills Unemployment or frequent job changes
Family structure	Young family Partner present 'Empty' relationship	Unstable, partner changes Violent relationships
Childhood of parents	Neglected	Maltreatment
Expectations	Low	Very high or nil 'Just want peace and quiet'
Network support	Poor	Poor relationships Isolated
Parental coping strategies	Withdrawal	Violent outbursts or withdrawal Punishment is an expression of frustration
Children	Passive in infancy Can be very active when older Developmental delay	Out of control
Prognosis	? Poor Limited skills and 'vision' of change	Variable

health refers to the differences that result from less access to health care and less opportunity for healthy living due to factors such as poor housing or diet. 'Neglect' refers to the standard of care delivered to the child, and covers such areas as failure to provide adequate food, to protect from danger, and/or to provide stimulation. Deprivation, as defined by the National Child Development Study (NCDS) publications, includes the 4.5% of familes where there is low income, poor housing and single parent or large families.[3] The term 'deprivation' is often used to describe both inequalities and neglect, which frequently go together and are difficult to dissect.

Poor nutrition where there are food shortages is a consequence of inequality; poor nutrition due to a failure to provide food when supplies are available is neglect. However, the families who fall into the latter category are also those more likely to have limited material and personal resources in terms of knowledge and their own health and emotional well-being. Simplistic approaches which might depend upon one type of intervention, such as providing more resources (aid, benefits, charity), punishment for wilful failure to provide care, education, or support and counselling, are likely to be less successful than a broad approach that acknowledges a wide range of causes. Inequalities and disadvantage also have a time axis, in that they are likely to extend over years and generations of the same families. Programmes for intervention, therefore, need to be long-term and sustained if there are to be benefits, and the outcome measures to be recorded may be distant in time from the intervention, e.g. educational attainment at age 16 or quality of parenting achieved by those whose parents were enrolled in the scheme.

Parental care and health interact with one another. In the model modified from Hutchison the quality of parenting is represented on the vertical axis (Fig. 2).[4] In each segment, the parental contribution towards preventing, limiting, increasing or causing ill health can be seen.

If the definition of neglect given above is used, neglect which has not yet led to a serious impairment may not be registered. It is the hallmark of community paediatrics that we wish to prevent these events from occurring. To take an example, a child *may* be left to play alone in a street, he *might* wander into the road and *might* be injured by a vehicle, and this injury *may* be minor, serious or fatal. How do we decide a dividing line for neglect? In this example, it might be decided by age, depending on whether the child is age 2, 5, 7 or 10, but some would argue that all these ages lack the skills to cross the road safely. Neglect therefore needs to take in a range of indicators such as the list used in Nottingham. This parallels the use of several indicators to define disadvantage in the NCDS.

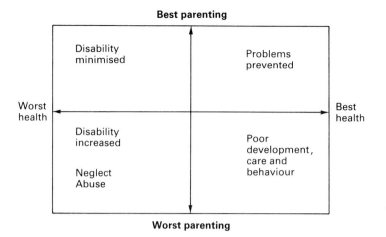

Best parenting

Disability minimised

Problems prevented

Worst health

Best health

Disability increased

Poor development, care and behaviour

Neglect Abuse

Worst parenting

Fig. 2.   *Interaction of parental care and child development (after Hutchinson[4]).*

Under the 1989 Children Act, a court may make a care or supervision order if it is satisfied that:

a. the child concerned is suffering or likely to suffer *significant* harm; and
b. that the harm, or likelihood of harm, is attributable to:
(i) the care given to the child, or likely to be given to him if the order were not made, not being what it would be *reasonable* to expect a parent to give to him; or
(ii) the child's being beyond parental control.

The difficulty for the paediatrician whose advice may be sought is in the definitions of 'significant' and 'reasonable'.

Prediction of child neglect

Factors that may predict neglect antenatally, at the six-week or subsequent checks are listed in Tables 2–5. These 'indicators' may be used to identify families who require more intensive support. A single indicator has little significance, but the presence of multiple factors should serve to highlight the extra needs of these families. Although a combination of risk factors may have both a specificity and sensitivity greater than 80%, they cannot be used as a screening test because far too many false positives would be found.[5] Browne *et al.* estimate that such a process applied to a population of 10,000 births would identify 33 out of 40 abusers, but also over 1,000 false positives. The indicators can, however, be used to guide professional judgements. The family characteristics of families who neglect, and both neglect and abuse their children are quite different. The features described by Crittenden are familiar to community paediatricians who work in deprived areas.[2]

Table 2. Items that may have predictive value antenatally

- Not living with father of baby
- History of 'in care' as a child
- Received special education for MLD or behavioural problems
- School attendance problems
- Moved house more than once during pregnancy
- Booked late or not booked
- Poor attendance at antenatal clinic
- Was abused as a child
- Smoking in pregnancy, with no intention to cut down
- Poor management of personal finances
- Has had social worker or probation officer
- History of violence
- Age 21 or under
- Older children abused or neglected
- Tattoos
- Psychiatric history, mental illness, drug or alcohol abuse

MLD = moderate learning difficulties

Table 3. Items that may have predictive value at the six-week check

---

- DNA
- Completed after three months of age
- A combination of the following:
  - failure to thrive
  - widespread ammoniacal dermatitis that has not been treated
  - described as naughty
  - dislikes being handled
  - 'disinterested handling'
  - rough or impatient handling
  - dirty clothing
  - mother noticed not to speak to child during check
  - mother noticed not to have direct eye contact with child
  - untreated or unrecognised infection
  - excessive crying or apathetic
  - difficult feeder
  - has not written in PHR
  - has ears pierced?

PHR = parent held record

Table 4. Later parental indicators/measures

- Failure to immunise
- DNA for surveillance checks
- Failure to write in PHR
- Safety hazards in the home that are persistent
- Left alone or inadequately supervised
- Lack of regular meal- and bedtimes
- No 'bedtime routine'
- No regular tooth cleaning
- Clothes dirty
- Clothes inappropriate for weather
- No playtime with parents
- No family mealtimes
- Failure to set simple clear rules
- Failure to intervene when child is in danger
- Failure to intervene when child's behaviour is poor
- Excessive, persistent and exclusive use of physical punishment
- Failure to recognise and reward good behaviour
- Does not smile at child
- Failure to cuddle: 'what would you do if he hurt himself?' = failure to comfort
- Late presentation of medical problems
- Very poor compliance with treatment
- Does not hold hand or restrain in street

PHR = parent held record

Table 5. Later child indicators/measures

- Failure to thrive
- Attends accident and emergency more than once in a year
- Withdrawn or persistently unhappy
- Does not follow simple rules that would be expected for a child of his age
- Swears, but general language development poor
- Destroys toys
- Destroys other things
- Injures animals
- Plays with matches
- Lack of 'own space', bed, box, etc.
- Violence

There are, of course, protective factors that prevent neglect taking place even where there are multiple risk factors. These may relate to positive experiences in childhood, better education, family, community or professional support.

Factors that influence child health, development and emotional well-being

The factors discussed below are those that influence the outcome for individual children. Some are capable of being changed by personal practice, others require action by local authorities or government and some, such as genetic factors, are not currently amenable to change. Graham adopts a 'bottom-line' approach in terms of a basic level of need and provision which, if not met, would lead to impairment in health.[6] He defines these as:

- adequate diet, housing and income;
- a stable, continuous source of affection and care, together with protection from physical, emotional and sexual abuse;
- cognitive stimulation and adequate education;
- safe environment;
- access to preventive and curative health care.

Genetics

Studies of families both of gifted children and of those with learning difficulties quoted by Rutter and Madge show strong intergenerational continuities.[7] In the Isle of Wight study, 37% of the families of children with learning difficulties had a family history of learning problems compared to 12% of the general population.[8]

Table 6. Children's health by housing conditions (from Platt *et al.*[10])

	No damp	Damp	Mould
Number of symptoms per child $p < 0.001$	2.04	2.46	2.86

Symptoms recorded included: aches and pains, diarrhoea, wheezing, vomiting, sore throat, irritability, tiredness, headaches, earache, fever, depression, tantrums, bedwetting, poor appetite, persistent cough, running nose.

Although it is difficult to dissect inherited factors from the care received from parents, there is a high correlation between the IQ of parents and children, even where they are reared away from their natural parents. We often talk about children reaching or failing to reach their 'full potential', and describe the improvements in development when children's circumstances are improved, for example, following a day nursery placement or, more radically, by removal from a deprived home and adoption into a privileged one. However, it is difficult, if not impossible, to predict the 'potential' of individuals and the degree of improvement to expect with improvements in care. The extent to which these levels of development can improve depends upon the age at which adverse conditions are removed.[9]

Environment

Housing. Housing conditions can have a profound effect upon children's health and development. Peaks of ill health and mortality in the winter months, which are a prominent feature in the UK, are probably related to dampness (Table 6)[10] and defects in heating and ventilation. It has been well-known since the earliest days of public health that overcrowding and poor sanitary conditions are related to the spread of infectious disease, particularly gastroenteritis and respiratory infections.[11] Passive smoking will add to the risks of acquiring respiratory infections and secretory otitis media. Poor housing is also associated with an increase in childhood accidents. Children living in flats or in other circumstances where there is no safe supervised play area, such as a private garden or playground, are likely to be at risk through playing outside on roads and other dangerous areas. Every year 25,000 children are admitted to hospital in the UK with accidents involving architectural features of their home.

Poor housing can lead to maternal depression and adverse effects upon child development. Overcrowding can lead to conflict within the home, and children can suffer from lack of personal privacy, which is especially important for teenagers, and lack of space and proper conditions to do homework.

Homelessness may result in inadequate housing in bed-and-breakfast accommodation, with very restricted facilities for play and preparing meals. Frequent moves provide stress for families, insecurity for children, and disrupt continuity of service provision in terms of changes of school, medical practitioner and social work support.[12]

Neighbourhoods. Community paediatricians are well aware that health is powerfully affected not only by the quality of individual houses, but also by the overall nature of the neighbourhood. Within a neighbourhood there are often associated problems of lack of local amenities, public transport, adequate refuse collections and shops. Blocks of flats may have particular problems with security and vandalism.[13]

Deprived neighbourhoods are also associated with increased unemployment and increases in juvenile crime.[14]

Health workers need therefore to be aware of local living conditions and the difficulties they may create for parents in bringing up their children.

Income and social class

Many indices of child health, such as growth, mortality rates, respiratory infections, hospital admissions and educational attainments have been related to income and social class. The problems of income and its appropriate utilisation have been discussed. Those on low income spend 30% of expenditure on food compared to those on high income, and are likely to provide a poorer quality diet for their children, with less fruit, fresh vegetables and fresh meat.[15,16]

Lack of disposable income provides extreme difficulties in budgeting in comparison with those who have large surpluses. Their skills in budgeting or getting value for money may not be sufficient to prevent families slipping into debt. For the families at the lowest income level, providing an adequate diet and remaining out of debt may be an impossibility. Debt or fear of debt may put large stresses on families. Poverty and its outward appearances may also have a detrimental effect on self esteem, and provide an obvious badge by which they can be identified by others.

Health workers therefore should be aware of the limitations placed upon child care by low income, and of the personal sensitivities related to poverty.

Family structure

Of every 1,000 live births 214 are illegitimate. Although 80% of children now live with both natural parents, one in three marriages ends in divorce, 56% of these couples having children under the age of 16. What are the effects of these differing family structures on children? Perinatal, neonatal and post-neonatal mortality rates are higher for illegitimate births, and educational attainments at age seven are poorer.[17] In practice, the difficulties children have may arise from a number of factors associated with family structure. These may be economic due to low income, secondary to the stress or depression that an unsupported parent may experience, or related to family tensions and arguments. Professional help may need to be focused at all three levels. Marital breakdown occurs more commonly in families where parents' childhoods were marked by divorce or separation. Skilled counselling is needed to explore family relationships with parents and children.

Culture

In the UK, there are higher perinatal and infant mortality rates for some immigrant groups. Part of this may relate to lower socio-economic status and part to inherited disease, particularly where there is consanguinity. Health workers are often faced with different child-rearing practices and family traditions, which they need to understand before acceptable advice can be given.[18,19] For example, understanding religious dietary restrictions or the contrasts between life-styles or living conditions in their country of origin and the UK can form a basis for explaining some medical problems such as iron deficiency, and for appreciating the degree of adaptation required to a new environment. Interpreters and link workers recruited from the community to promote health care and explain customs are an essential part of the service to immigrant communities.

Stimulation

Children can learn only as a result of the stimulation they receive. Lack of early stimulation results in impaired language development and later educational difficulties. Bath found significant language delay in up to 50% of children attending social-service day nurseries in Nottingham.[20] Interventions may involve general advice to parents on the importance of language stimulation, the introduction of language programmes or help for underlying problems such as parental depression which may impair communication. Pollak found poor levels of development associated with inadequate stimulation from child minders in South London.[21]

Nurture and affection

Bonding is a powerful, specific attachment between parents and child that enables care, protection, affection, sacrifice and empathy to take place. Its origins are in the parents' own child-rearing experience. It is facilitated by early contact between mother and child, and is inhibited by separations, malformations or unresponsiveness of the child, or adverse circumstances such as an unwanted pregnancy. Children who do not receive affection, and whose parents are consistently critical are likely to suffer low self esteem and severe emotional problems. Facilitation and understanding of positive reactions between parents and children are important in the prevention and management of these behaviour problems. Children in early life are often withdrawn (though often later having more outwardly difficult behaviour), they fail to thrive and have characteristically cold extremities (deprivation hands and feet).

Diet

Non-organic growth delay is associated with developmental delay as
shown by Dowdney *et al.* in a study of four-year-olds from an inner-city
area.[22] Children whose weight and height lay below the tenth centile
were found to have a general cognitive index of 77.1 compared to 97.7
for controls. Two per cent of the Caucasian inner-city children fitted
their definition of chronic non-organic growth retardation, and 35%
of these had a cognitive index below 70 points. In these children, an
inadequate diet was the main cause of their failure to thrive. In
Nottingham inner-city children, overall 25% were iron-deficient at
15–24 months, with a rate of 39% in Asian children.[23] In Birmingham, Grindulis *et al.* found that two-fifths of Asian toddlers were
vitamin D-deficient.[24] Treatment of iron-deficient children in Birmingham led to improved weight gain, and 42% of the children whose
haemoglobin rose by 2 g or more as a result of treatment achieved six
or more new skills on the Denver scale compared to 13% in controls.[25]
There are conflicting claims for improvement in IQ by giving vitamin
and mineral supplements to schoolchildren.[26]

Clearly, poor nutrition is common in a relatively wealthy country
such as the UK, and is associated with poor development. Causes,
however, may be complex and can relate to low income, inadequate
knowledge about diet or, as described by Skuse, a maladaptive
behavioural interaction between care-giver and infant, sustained by
high emotional tensions.[27] Barker and Osmond have suggested that
poor nutrition in childhood may have long-term consequences in the
incidence of ischaemic heart disease in adult life.[28]

In the Jamaican study the effects upon development both of
nutritional supplementation and of stimulation were investigated in
stunted children, age 9–24 months.[29] The authors were able to
demonstrate the relationship between these two factors. The developmental quotient (DQ) improved for stimulated and supplemented
children, but not in controls. Children who received both supplementation and stimulation did better than children who received only a
single intervention. Children who received both interventions had a
mean DQ 13.4 points higher than controls after 24 months; with
improvements of 6.5 and 7.9 points for single interventions.

Access to child welfare services

Access to adequate child welfare services is not equal. Parents in
disadvantaged areas face difficulties if they do not have a telephone to
contact the doctor or personal transport to bring their child to clinic

or surgery. Children from disadvantaged families are certainly much more likely to be admitted to hospital for preventable causes of ill health.[30-32] This may be related to the ability to prevent or recognise ill health as well as to decision making with regard to medical consultation and access to health care.

Life events

Life events in a child's family may have profound effects upon the overall functioning of the family. Obvious examples are the death of or the onset of disability in a parent. Unemployment, housing problems, family separations, convictions or being a victim of crime are also important. Life events can of course be positive as well as adverse: 'he hasn't looked back since . . .'. Medical records may have life-event lists, which can usefully supplement problem lists and other summary sheets.

Temperament

Children of similar levels of intelligence, given the same opportunities and the same quality of care, do not always reach the same outcomes. An important factor is the individual child's temperament,[33] important characteristics of which may be drive, adaptability to change, persistence, distractability, regularity of behaviours such as sleeping, and thresholds of responsiveness. The child's temperament needs to match or be compatible with the life-styles and expectations of the rest of the family. For example, a child who is quiet and thoughtful may be of concern in a family whose general characteristics are boisterous and outgoing. In others, an 'average' child born into a quiet and thoughtful family may be viewed as hyperactive. Assessment of individual children and their families must take temperament into account, and also recognise that our own individual temperaments may also influence our judgement at times.

Early intervention schemes

The association between adverse factors and child development has been discussed. This section deals with community programmes designed to prevent the consequences of disadvantage, or at least to minimise its effects. These aims are central to any 'mission statement' about community paediatric services. Research to demonstrate the effectiveness of these programmes is difficult, in that it is not easy to secure sufficient numbers of children and long enough follow-up to demonstrate outcomes.

Pre-school education: nursery school, day nursery and playgroup

The effects of pre-school experience in these settings were investigated by Osborn and Milbank in the Child Health and Education study of a cohort of 13,000 children born in 1970.[34] They found better attainments in the children who had received pre-school education. Children who attended nursery schools and playgroups did best, and children from disadvantaged families did best when they attended nursery schools. Children who had attended day nurseries had the poorest attainments in reading and mathematics.

This important study should influence community health workers to advocate both the availability and uptake of pre-school education. It also indicates the importance of pre-school education for disadvantaged groups, and the need to improve educational provision in day nurseries.

Family centres

Family centres are designed for both parents and children. They provide support for parents, but also education in child care and an important element of 'parenting of the parents'. The aims of the Radford Family Centre were to:

- promote practical parenting skills;
- promote better home management;
- promote literacy;
- provide insight for parents into the needs of children, both in family life and in education;
- promote satisfaction for parents in parenting, and enjoyment of their children;
- reduce dependence on agencies for day-to-day care and acute problems.[35]

The centre was staffed by a multidisciplinary team, which included a social worker, a nursery teacher, a playgroup leader and a health visitor. Additional help was obtained from adult literacy teachers, a cook (who also taught) and a hairdresser.

Some family centres work with families with severe multiple problems, or where there has been child abuse. For example, of 22 parents attending the Radford Family Centre, 14 had literacy problems, of whom 9 received special education, 13 had previous court appearances, 11 had been in care as children, and 7 had psychiatric problems. Work in the centre included individual reviews and counselling, a daily rota organised for tasks such as washing up and serving food and group work and practical activities including health education, budgeting, literacy, child care, play, family life, bereavement, and cooking. The focus of work was on decision making, self help and personal responsibility as well as the acquisition of knowledge and skills. Improvements in self esteem and in self care and appearance were important elements in the functioning of the centre.

Results have been variable: ten years later some children are in care, but other families are performing much better, with no special professional involvement and with their children making normal physical, emotional and developmental progress.

High Scope Perry pre-school programme (Figs. 3 and 4)

In the Perry pre-school programme in the USA, children whose mothers had been engaged in an early intervention programme when their children were infants were found to have better educational attainments and chances of employment on leaving school, and less chance of being in care or in trouble with the law.[36] The crucial features were an early start and parental involvement. The programme involved weekly home visits and a daily pre-school programme extending over two years. The authors in this study were also able to demonstrate that their programmes were cost-effective. They estimated that for each $1,000 invested in the programme, $4,130 would be returned to society because of the costs that would otherwise have been associated with juvenile crime, special education and unemployment. The authors conclude that the child-positive attitudes and increased parental aspirations were important factors in the success of the programme.

Cope Street Centre

Referrals to the Cope Street Centre in Nottingham's inner city are mainly teenage parents.[37] The core staff are health-based, consisting of a health visitor, a midwife and nursery nurses. The programmes at Cope Street centre around parents defining their own needs, and groups and topics chosen by parents are set up. Increasing self-confidence has been an important theme in the work of the centre. The staff recognise that parents may learn more from others in the same situation than from traditional teaching by health professionals. They also stress that people learn by doing: hence the practical activities in the centre. Parents are involved in the planning, organisation and evaluation of group sessions. The groups include those for teenage antenatal and teenage mothers, food, the Open University (using the Open University courses for parents), crafts, coping with kids, and a literacy summer school.

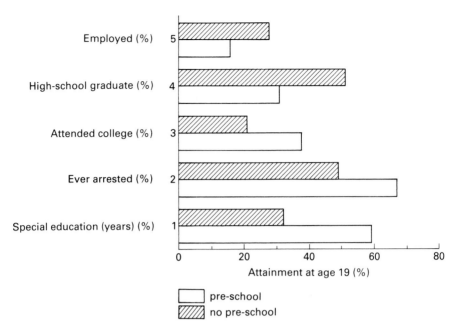

Fig. 3. *Findings at 19 years in the High Scope Perry pre-school programme.*

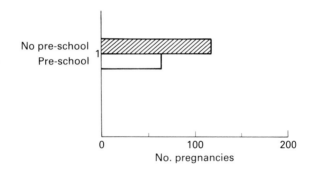

Fig. 4. *Number of teenage pregnancies per 100 females in High Scope Perry study at age 19.*

The approach of Cope Street has been most successful. Examples of achievements have been:

- all the members of the Open University group going on to college;
- the teenage mothers' group giving talks in local secondary schools, and featuring on a local radio programme;
- the food group producing their own cookery book;
- groups addressing meetings of health visitors and midwives;
- the 'coping with kids' group continuing to meet in one another's houses after the group at the centre had finished.

Cope Street and other similar centres break away from the mould of conventional health-service provision. They provide a much more intensive service than is available from routine programmes, and a message and medium acceptable to their target group. Short-term follow-up has suggested that the programmes can not only impart knowledge and skills but overcome the consequences of the parents' own deprived childhoods and emotional needs, and also the difficulty of combining adolescence with parenthood.

Bristol child development programme

The child development programme at Bristol has been developed by the Early Childhood Development Unit at the University of Bristol.[38] This is a structured programme carried out by specially trained health visitors, and includes a system for monitoring of results. It is focused on first-time parents, usually during the antenatal period and the first eight months of life, but can be extended up to the age of three years. The parents receive more frequent home visits, and the health visitor uses attractive cartoon-style materials that encourage parents to develop their own skills rather than be a passive receptacle for advice. Important issues covered are early health, nutrition, language, social-isation, early education and parents' own health and self esteem.

The programme claims increased parental self esteem, improved diet and immunisation rates, reduced hospitalisation of children, and greater job satisfaction for health visitors. More research is needed to confirm these results and to see how much of these improvements are due to more health visiting, to the programme or to the selection of the health visitors who carry it out.

Language schemes

Language delay is a common finding among children in disadvan-taged families. For this reason, language programmes have been developed to prevent language delay or to manage children from the groups already affected. Bath developed the use of language pro-grammes in day nurseries by nursery nurses.[20] She used programmes developed along the lines of the Wolfson developmental language programme.[39] This follows a sequence through attention control, comprehension and symbolic understanding, to expression. Assessment preceded enrolment on the programme and careful records were kept on each child. Results show rapid progress in the majority of children, and maintenance of a normal rate of language development one year after their involvement in the programme ended.

The Burnley, Pendle and Rossendale language programme was

developed in 1983 by the speech therapy department of the local health authority.[40] It is designed for use with groups of children in day nurseries and comprises five daily topics covering eight weeks. The programme is prepared on two levels to meet individual abilities, and is designed for children who are linguistically deprived rather than those who have specific language problems. Examples of the topics covered are:

- name and use of common objects;
- listening and attention (sound sequences, rhythm, stories);
- classification (identifying like or related objects, e.g. cups, spoons, books on shelf, coat on hooks, bricks by colour);
- action day (demonstrating use of objects, identifying objects by mime);
- positioning (understanding use of 'on', 'under', 'in' etc.);
- size and shape; and
- sequencing (e.g. putting objects in requested order).

This programme is now used throughout the day nurseries in Nottingham.

Portage

The Portage scheme was developed in Portage, Wisconsin, as a home-based scheme to help the development of pre-school children with moderate learning difficulties.[41] It is widely used in the UK and other countries. A trained portage worker visits the family for about an hour a week. A developmental checklist covering social, language, cognitive, self-help and motor skills is filled out by the parent and portage worker. Targets are then chosen and broken down into stages with a series of activities that can be completed within the week. The portage materials include cards with suggestions for activities that will lead towards the target. The portage worker shows the parent each stage of the programme, including important techniques such as reinforcement, and also observes the parents carrying it out. Progress records are kept by the parents, so that skill levels before and after teaching are known. The system works well with children whose developmental delay is related to their deprived background as well as those with intrinsic causes for their learning difficulties.

Iron deficiency

Intervention programmes may also successfully target important clinical problems. James *et al.* set up a programme of education and screening to reduce iron deficiency in an inner-city general practice.[42] Dietary information was provided antenatally and in the first year of life. An information sheet on foods rich in iron, including those suitable for vegetarians, was given to all mothers. Haemoglobin was measured at the time of measles, mumps, rubella (MMR) immunisation in the second year of life. Iron deficiency in the practice dropped from 25% to 8% following the introduction of the education programme. This study conducted from a general practice, is a demonstration of the effectiveness of a community-based nutrition education programme.

References

1. Children Act 1989. *Working paper* no. 22. London: HMSO, 1991
2. Crittenden P. Family and dyadic patterns of functioning in maltreating families. In: Browne K, Davies C, Stratton P, eds. *Early prediction and prevention of child abuse.* Chichester: John Wiley and Sons, 1988
3. Wedge P, Prosser H. *Born to fail.* London: Arrow Books, 1973
4. Hutchison TP. (unpublished material)
5. Browne K, Davies C, Strattan P, eds. *Early prediction and prevention of child abuse.* Chichester: John Wiley and Son, 1988
6. Graham P. Social class, social disadvantage and child health. *Child Soc* 1988; **2**: 9–19
7. Rutter M, Madge N. *Cycles of disadvantage.* London: Heinemann, 1976
8. Rutter M, Tizard J, Whitmore K. *Education, health and behaviour.* London: Longman, 1970
9. Rutter M. The long-term effects of early experience. *Dev Med Child Neurol* 1980; **22**: 800–15
10. Platt SD, Martin CJ, Hunt SM, Lewis SW. Damp housing, mould growth, and symptomatic health state. *Br Med J* 1989; **298**: 1673–8
11. Lowry S. *Housing and health.* London: British Medical Journal Books, 1991
12. Edwards R. *Homeless families (highlight no. 99).* London: National Children's Bureau, 1991
13. Coleman A. *Utopia on trial: vision and reality in planned housing.* London: Hilary Shipman, 1985
14. Nottingham County Council. *County deprivation study,* 1983
15. Sheppard J. *Food facts.* London: London Food Commission, 1986
16. Graham H, Stacey M. Socioeconomic factors related to child health. In: MacFarlane JA, ed. *Progress in child health, vol. 1.* London: Churchill Livingstone, 1984
17. Crellin E, Pringle ML, West P. *Born illegitimate. Social and educational implications.* Windsor: NFER, 1971
18. Henley A. *Asian patients at home and at hospital.* London: The King's Fund, 1979
19. Black J. *Child health in a multicultural society.* London: British Medical Journal Books, 1990
20. Bath D. Developing the speech therapy service in day nurseries: a progress report. *Br J Disord Communication* 1981; **16**: 159–73
21. Pollak M. *Nine year olds.* Lancaster: MTP Press, 1979
22. Dowdney L, Skuse D, Hepstinstall E, Puckering C, Zur-Szpiro S. Growth retardation and developmental delay amongst inner-city children. *J Child Psychiatry Child Psychol* 1987; **28**: 529–41
23. Marder E, Nicoll A, Polnay L, Shulman CE. Discovering anaemia at child health clinics. *Arch Dis Child* 1990; **65**: 892–4
24. Grindulis H, Scott PH, Belton NR, Wharton BA. Combined deficiency of iron and vitamin D in Asian toddlers. *Arch Dis Child* 1986; **61**: 843–8
25. Aukett A, Parks YA, Scott PH, Wharton BA. Treatment with iron increases weight gain and psychomotor development. *Arch Dis Child* 1986; **61**: 849–57
26. Whitehead RE. Vitamins, minerals, schoolchildren and IQ. *Br Med J* 1991; **302**: 548

27. Skuse DH. Non-organic failure to thrive: a reappraisal. *Arch Dis Child* 1985; **60**: 173–8
28. Barker DJP, Osmond C. Infant mortality, childhood nutrition and ischaemic heart disease in England and Wales. *Lancet* 1986; **ii**: 1077–81
29. Grantham-McGregor SM, Powell CA, Walker SP, Himes JH. Nutritional supplementation, and mental development of stunted children: the Jamaican study. *Lancet* 1991; **338**: 1–5
30. Wynne J, Hull D. Why are children admitted to hospital? *Br Med J* 1977; **2**: 1140–2
31. Carter EP, Drew AG, Thomas ME, Mohan JF, Savage MO, Larcher VF. Material deprivation and its association with childhood hospital admission in the East End of London. *Matern Child Health* 1990; **15**: 183–6
32. Conway SP, Phillips RR, Panday S. Admission to hospital with gastroenteritis *Arch Dis Child* 1990; **65**: 579–84
33. Oberklaid F. The clinical assessment of temperament in infants and young children. *Matern Child Health* 1991; **16**: 14–7
34. Osborn AF, Milbank JE. *The effect of early education: a report of the child health and education study.* Oxford: Oxford University Press, 1987
35. Polnay L. A service for problem families. *Arch Dis Child* 1985; **60**: 887–90
36. Schweindart LJ, Weihart DP. Young children grow up. The effects of the Perry pre-school programme on youth through age 15. *Monographs of High Scope Educational Research Programme, no. 7.* Ypsilanti MI: High Scope Education & Research Foundation, 1980
37. Billingham K. 45 Cope Street: working in partnership with parents. *Health Visitor* 1989; **62**: 156–7
38. Barker W. *Child development programme.* University of Bristol: School of Applied Social Sciences, 1984
39. Cooper J, Moodley M, Reynell J. *Helping language development.* London: Edward Arnold, 1978
40. *Speech therapy language programme.* Burnley, Pendle and Rossendale Health Authority, 1984
41. Cameron RJ, ed. *Working together: Portage in the UK.* Windsor: NFER-Nelson, 1982
42. James J, Lawson P, Male P, Oakhill A. Preventing iron deficiency in preschool children by implementing an educational and screening programme in an inner city practice *Br Med J* 1989; **299**: 838–40

Further reading

1. Black D. *Inequalities in health. Report of a research working group.* London: Department of Health and Social Security, 1980
2. Blaxter M. The health of the children. A review of research on the place of health in cycles of disadvantage. *Social Science Research Council/Department of Health and Social Security. Studies in deprivation and disadvantage 3.* London: Heinemann, 1981
3. Dowling S. *Health for a change.* London: Child Poverty Action Group, 1983
4. Rutter M, Maughan B, Mortimore P, Ouston J. *Fifteen thousand hours.* London: Open Books, 1979
5. Syla K. Does early intervention work? *Arch Dis Child* 1989; **64**: 1103–4
6. Wedge P, Essen J. *Children in adversity.* London: Pan Books, 1982
7. Whitehead M. *The health divide: inequalities in health in the 1980s.* London: Health Education Authority, 1987
8. Wicks M. Family trends, insecurities and social policy. *Child Soc* 1989; **3**: 67–80

13 | Injury and accident prevention: achievements and challenges

Ivan Pless

Professor of Pediatrics, Epidemiology and Biostatistics, McGill University
Director, Community Pediatric Research Programme, McGill-Montreal
Children's Hospital Research Institute, Montreal, Canada

Introduction

It is a formidable task to provide a suitable conclusion for such a broad-ranging publication. On the one hand, each chapter is impressive and deserves careful consideration. On the other hand, not all the matters which, in my view, needed to be raised have been addressed, or have not been dealt with in sufficient depth. This chapter is primarily intended, therefore, to highlight several of these issues.

To start with a provocative statement may be unwise but it is, none the less, a fair summary of the situation at present. In my judgement, there is little evidence that Britain is, as yet, determined to conquer the epidemic of accidents and injuries in childhood. Although this is a serious charge, I believe it withstands scrutiny. It arises from my personal perspective, that of a Canadian who has spent much of his professional life in the USA and, accordingly, views challenges and achievements with respect to injury control in a broad international context. I will focus primarily on the present situation in Britain, but many of the most important observations seem widely applicable. They pertain in particular to Canada and the USA as well as many European countries, with the notable exception of Scandinavia.

Three principal areas will be cited in which there have been remarkable achievements but where serious challenges remain:

- declining mortality rates;
- scientific accomplishments; and
- increased visibility.

Declining mortality rates

One outstanding achievement of the last decade is that the mortality rate for injuries has continued to decline. The word 'continued' is important, however, because it must be appreciated that the downward trend in child mortality from injuries and accidents in Britain actually began much earlier than 1980. As indicated in Fig. 1, the rise between 1931 and 1941 was followed by a sharp decline that began to level out in the mid-1950s. That it has continued, albeit at a slower rate, is encouraging, but clearly caution is needed.

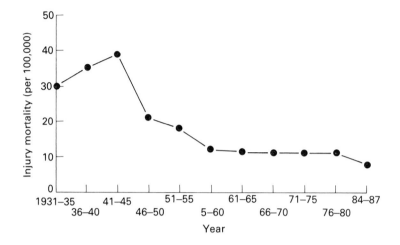

Fig. 1. *Injury mortality, ages 1–14 years, England and Wales.*

Similar improvements have been seen in most Western countries since 1955. Figure 2 shows the rates of change between 1955 and 1985 for boys aged 1–4 in 9 countries, expressed as percentages of the rates per 100,000 in 1955. The figures indicate that some countries are improving at a much faster rate than Britain, while others are much slower. The contrast between England & Wales and Sweden over the period 1966–88, again using rates for boys aged 1–4 years, is particularly instructive (Fig. 3).

Another comparison with similar countries, based on 1985 rates also presents a reasonably favourable picture (Fig. 4). Although total mortality rates (all causes and ages combined) may appear impressive when compared with those in, say, Canada, the USA or Australia, the picture for specific causes of death, or for deaths in certain age groups, is less comforting, as the following example shows. In Fig. 5, rates per 100,000 for boys in each of four age groups are given for deaths from poisoning, burns and scalds, and drownings. It is evident that the patterns are very different, and would be even greater if additional comparisons for girls were shown.

Therefore, whether declining mortality and some favourable overall comparative rates are viewed as an achievement or a challenge depends on how we view half empty and half full glasses. The challenge is to do better and to bring Britain's rates into line with those of other similar countries. Of equal importance is to remove disparities between regions within the country. These variations chiefly reflect socio-economic factors, but this does not mean that the only solution lies with the seemingly impossible dream of eliminating poverty. It simply means that regions with high mortality rates require a greater share of resources so that they can implement prevention programmes that have been proven to be effective.

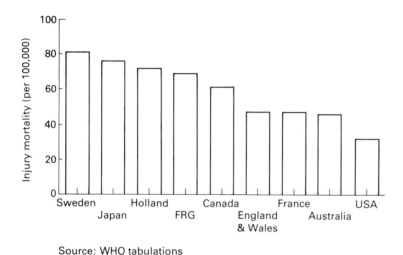

Source: WHO tabulations

Fig. 2. *Percentage change in injury rates, boys 1–4 years, selected countries, 1955–1985 (expressed as percentages of the rates per 100,000 deaths in 1955).*

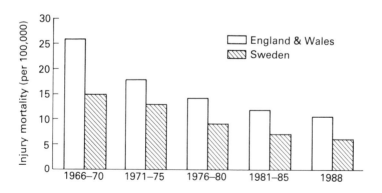

Fig. 3. *Comparative injury mortality, boys 1–4 years, rates per 100,000.*

Scientific accomplishments

The second main area of accomplishment encompasses the set of discoveries that are likely to be related to the steadily improving rates described above. These preventive measures are the fruits of scientific achievements—often technological—in a large number of areas. Table 1 lists some that have been formally evaluated, together with figures (in many instances approximations) intended to illustrate what some studies have shown can be accomplished under optimal circumstances by one or more of the preventive tactics listed—that is, the efficacy of the manoeuvre. What happens in the real world has rarely been studied, but it appears, almost invariably, to be far less.

As Table 1 shows, the applications are diverse, but several patterns deserve comment. First, that few of these 'breakthroughs' lie in the field of *primary prevention*, that is, in preventing the accident itself. An important exception is child-resistant containers which, both in theory and in practice, prevent ingestion, and consequently have almost eliminated deaths among children from substances so packaged.[1]

Table 1. The prevention gap: efficacy vs. effectiveness

Prevention tactic	Efficacy (%)	Level of use (%)
Safety seats and belts	80	40–80
Bicycle helmets	88	5
Pedestrian walkways	30 ?	5 ??
Smoke detectors	85 ?	20
Hot-water heaters	90 ?	20
Tap-water regulators	90	5
Window guards	90	10 ??
Stair guards	70 ?	25
Pool enclosures	80	20 ??

Most of those listed, however, lie in the domain of *secondary prevention*, where the effect of the manoeuvre is to prevent or minimise injury following the initial hazardous event. The introduction of seat restraints is perhaps the best known example, and several careful evaluation studies have proven their value beyond any doubt.[2]

Finally, an important component of the decline in mortality may well be attributable to *tertiary prevention*. This refers to the effectiveness of services provided following an actual injury, but which serve to diminish the consequences of that event. The work of accident and emergency departments or trauma centres, illustrates this approach. Unfortunately, few of these have been carefully evaluated, but it is

difficult to imagine that they have not saved scores of lives and thus
contributed substantially to the favourable statistics.

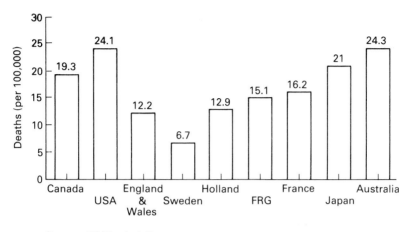

Source: WHO tabulations

Fig. 4. *Death rates, all injuries, boys 10–14 years, selected countries, 1985.*

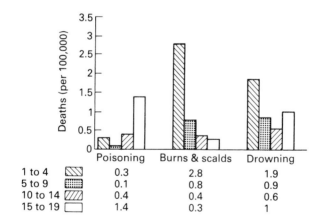

		Poisoning	Burns & scalds	Drowning
1 to 4		0.3	2.8	1.9
5 to 9		0.1	0.8	0.9
10 to 14		0.4	0.4	0.6
15 to 19		1.4	0.3	1

Fig. 5. *Injury mortality by type, boys rates per 100,000, England and Wales, 1984–86.*

Secondary prevention strategies

One common element in the large number of secondary prevention
strategies that have been evaluated is that the most efficacious are
often built around 'devices' that require only a single action or
relatively few repetitions of a preventive behaviour. Figure 6 illustrates
the passive–active principle as it relates to poisoning: the more frequently an action is required (for example, having to return dangerous

substances to a locked cabinet after every use) the less the likelihood of prevention. In contrast, both the use of child-resistant containers and of packaging that restricts the contents to subtoxic doses greatly enhance the likelihood of success.

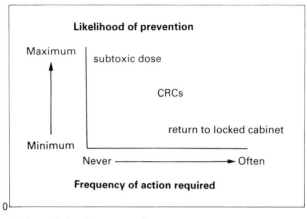

CRC = child resistant container

Fig. 6. *The passive–active principle.*

Another example is the bicycle helmet which usually needs to be 'installed' only once for each trip, as is the case with seat belts and safety seats. There are, however, sharp differences between these two examples that raise important questions about the logic of safety policy—or lack thereof. Seat belts and child safety seats are required by law, but bicycle helmets are not. The law requires not only that seat belts be used but also, very importantly, that automobile manufacturers install them. Furthermore, it is difficult, and in most countries illegal, to remove them. In contrast, helmets are not provided as part of standard equipment when buying a bicycle, which may be viewed as analogous to selling it without brakes. Hence, one important step would be to insist that helmets be included in the purchase price of bicycles. Another, less intrusive step is to include tags on bicycles that caution the purchaser that 'an essential part'—the helmet—is lacking. A third logical strategy is to legislate helmet use for the same sound reasons as restraint use is required.

The examples shown in Table 1 are accompanied by the good and bad news. The good news is, of course, that they have been shown to be efficacious; the bad news is that their effectiveness is invariably much less in practice, so the challenge in this area is to find ways to ensure that all children receive the full benefit of each of the accomplishments.

Increasing visibility

Another important achievement of the past decade is that injury prevention in childhood now has far more visibility. The general level of awareness of the lay public appears to have increased considerably, and the work of various safety groups also appears more sophisticated.

At the professional level, that a meeting has taken place under Royal College of Physicians auspices is itself an encouraging sign. It seems entirely likely that not too long ago the College would have resisted, arguing that accident prevention is only marginally a medical problem. The message about the importance of injury prevention also appears to be sinking in at government level, albeit perhaps far too slowly. None the less, it was gratifying to find injury prevention identified as a possible priority in the Secretary of State's Consultative Document.[3]

Thus, it appears that Britain is not too far behind in achieving the visibility for injury prevention that is an essential prerequisite for concerted and emphatic action. There is, however, little reason for complacency because Britain still lags far behind Sweden in particular, as well as perhaps the USA, in achieving the level of visibility for injury prevention in all the arenas where it is needed. For example, although some key people now agree that injuries among children are of epidemic proportions, there are many others who remain sceptical or simply ignorant of the facts.

The public, the media and many professional groups are too often startled to learn the size of the problem, and some still refuse to accept that it is truly a medical issue. They doubt that accident prevention can be studied scientifically or that many of the tragic events can be avoided with little effort. As is the case for the other areas cited, growing awareness remains part achievement and part challenge.

A special case for children

There is a fourth component that is almost entirely challenge. There appears to have been little progress in awareness that children are not simply small adults and that, accordingly, strategies to prevent childhood injuries demand special considerations. Although many of the most important preventive approaches apply to all age groups, there are a number of exceptional components. One is the disproportionate rate of occurrence of certain types of injuries according to each age group and, as in the elderly, the relatively more serious nature of injuries of most kinds. The special vulnerability of children, not only in the physical sense, but also as a reflection of their developmental immaturity, is still not well appreciated.

Too many safety experts assume that children are capable of being as responsive to cautionary messages and careful instructions as are adults. The assumption that health education alone can be effective in this regard has been disproved, and safety programmes must take this into account.[4] The fact is that young children depend on others, especially their parents, for their protection. Because this is true, it is essential to examine objectively how effective parents may reasonably be expected to be in this role, especially when the family lives in disadvantaged circumstances. Unfortunately, the view is still prevalent in some sectors in Britain (fostered by a misdirected emphasis on the role of family versus government) that the family alone is the source of, and solution to, most problems affecting children—a view that is scientifically unsupportable, and when taken to extremes is counter-productive and offensive to most parents.

Possible solutions to the challenges

It seems wrong to emphasise these challenges without suggesting some ways by which they could be overcome. Three stages are required:

- to implement measures that have been proven to be efficacious;
- to modify priorities so as to ensure that the resources required are made available; and
- to build powerful coalitions.

The last step is needed because the preceding ones each involve political action, and it is likely that pressure will be needed to persuade government to take that action. The principal step is to discover the means to apply fully what is already known, and to learn how to do so in an efficient, well co-ordinated manner. This is an interesting intellectual exercise: there is what amounts to a proven remedy for a disease, yet a failure to use it. How can this be explained?

The answer can be either simple or complex. The complex answer is that injury control is but one of a large variety of situations where the adoption of measures proven by research to be efficacious still requires that society work its way through a convoluted process that remains poorly understood. Dissemination of the basic knowledge is but the first, and no doubt easiest, stage of this process. Possessing information does not invariably lead to changes in behaviour, which is as true for physicians and health planners as for parents and children. Even a clear decision to implement a programme does not lead directly to all the needed changes, and frequently the time lag between such a decision and the changes is much longer than implementers expect.

The route to change is so circuitous partly because in many, perhaps most, instances the process of adoption, dissemination and implementation requires some form of political action. Without this, change may still take place but much more slowly and often in a haphazard manner.

To try to emulate the success of countries such as Sweden, Holland and, more recently, the USA in formulating injury control programmes for children it will probably be necessary to centralise responsibility for injury prevention. Logically, this should be placed only in the Ministry of Health. A desirable and possibly necessary additional step may require that a branch of the Ministry be created to deal exclusively with the childhood aspects of accident and injury prevention.

Coalition building

As has been stated, to achieve these goals is likely to require some means to form an effective coalition. This includes a wide array of health professionals, government officials and representatives of voluntary groups and agencies. Health professionals—accident and emergency consultants, public health officers, health visitors, paediatricians and surgeons—must certainly share a concern about accident prevention. It seems, however, that they may not speak the same language and, not surprisingly, rarely meet to share views on this issue. Only the Royal College of Physicians' meeting and another in Newcastle in 1991 have provided some opportunity to do so. Voluntary bodies often provide competing services, and as yet there is no means to ensure that their efforts are properly co-ordinated. Additionally, there are at least eight branches of central government that have a role in accident prevention, but they too rarely share ideas or resources to achieve the common objective.

Conclusion

The overriding and most immediate challenge remains that of conveying to the public, to politicians, and even to physicians and surgeons, not simply the magnitude of the injury problem, but also the enormous potential for their prevention. All the statistics describing the morbidity, mortality, disability, handicap, disfigurement and costs associated with injuries are readily susceptible to improvement. There is, however, not much evidence that Britain is approaching this problem with the seriousness and resolve it requires. There is little leadership and little co-ordination. If resources were no problem there might be only slight harm in the duplication of effort that arises from this situation. But, sadly, resources *are* a problem, and no country can afford the financial or intellectual luxury of struggling with such a large problem in such an inefficient manner.

The ultimate solution is remarkably simple: it is to find the political will to adopt solutions that are known to work. No one can seriously doubt that if the Secretary of State truly wished it, Britain would now have (as parts of Australia do) a bicycle helmet law, car seat legislation that is vigorously enforced, smoke detectors in every home, hot-water temperature regulators on every tap to which small children are exposed, and safe surfaces and safe equipment on playgrounds. The list is not endless, but it is certainly lengthy. All these items fall into the gap between what we know and what we do. The ultimate challenge is to bridge this gap quickly and completely.

References

1. Lawson GR, Craft AW, Jackson RH. Changing pattern of poisoning in children in Newcastle 1974–81. *Br Med J* 1983; **287**: 15–6
2. Agran PF, Dunkle DE, Winn DG. Effects of legislation on motor vehicle injuries to children. *Am J Dis Child* 1987; **141**: 949–64
3. Pless IB. Accident prevention. *Br Med J* 1991: **303**: 462–4
4. Pless IB, Arsenault L. The role of health education in the prevention of injuries to children. *J Social Issues* 1987; **43**: 87–103